# A Shamanic Way:
RITUALS, RATTLES, AND RECIPES FOR AWAKENING YOUR INNER SPIRIT.

PENNY RANDALL

Art by *Penelope*

BALBOA
PRESS
A DIVISION OF HAY HOUSE

Copyright © 2012–2014 Penny Randall

All rights reserved. No part of this book may be used or reproduced by any means, graphic, electronic, or mechanical, including photocopying, recording, taping or by any information storage retrieval system without the written permission of the publisher except in the case of brief quotations embodied in critical articles and reviews.

Art by Penelope

Balboa Press books may be ordered through booksellers or by contacting:

Balboa Press
A Division of Hay House
1663 Liberty Drive
Bloomington, IN 47403
www.balboapress.com
1-(877) 407-4847

ISBN: 978-1-4525-6499-9 (sc)
ISBN: 978-1-4525-6501-9 (hc)
ISBN: 978-1-4525-6500-2 (e)

Because of the dynamic nature of the Internet, any web addresses or links contained in this book may have changed since publication and may no longer be valid. The views expressed in this work are solely those of the author and do not necessarily reflect the views of the publisher, and the publisher hereby disclaims any responsibility for them.

The author of this book does not dispense medical advice or prescribe the use of any technique as a form of treatment for physical, emotional, or medical problems without the advice of a physician, either directly or indirectly. The intent of the author is only to offer information of a general nature to help you in your quest for emotional and spiritual well-being. In the event you use any of the information in this book for yourself, which is your constitutional right, the author and the publisher assume no responsibility for your actions.

Any people depicted in stock imagery provided by Thinkstock are models, and such images are being used for illustrative purposes only.
Certain stock imagery © Thinkstock.

Printed in the United States of America

Library of Congress Control Number: 2012923419
Balboa Press rev. date: 10/22/2014

> Dedicated to You, dear reader,
> our students,
> and everyone
> making an effort
> to learn something new
> to grow and succeed and
> to be all you were created to be.

Contents

Prologue xi

1. **TO BEGIN WITH** 1
   A Shaman's World by *Penelope* (Illustration) 2
   What is Shamanism and 'A Shamanic Way'? 9
   A Shamanic Way by *Penelope* (Illustration) 10
   Shamanic Healing, Soul Retrieval, Extraction and Cord Cutting 13

2. **SACRED TOOLS** 19
   Sacred Smoke by *Penelope* (Illustration) 20
   Sacred Smoke – Smudging 21
   Ritual 1   Smudging 24
   Other Medicine Smudge Plants 26
   Sacred Space / Sacred Tools by *Penelope* (Illustration) 30
   Sacred Tools 31
   Methods for Cleansing Sacred Tools 31
   Creating a Dedicated Sacred Space 32

3. **CREATING SACRED CIRCLE** 37
   Sacred Circle by *Penelope* (Illustration) 38
   Recipe 1 – Sacred Circle – Simple Example 42
   Recipe 2 – Sacred Circle – Elegant Example 44

4. **CALLING IN THE DIRECTIONS – Invocation** 49
   Sacred Directions by *Penelope* (Illustration) 50
   Ritual 2   Simple – Calling In 56
   Ritual 3   Elegant – Calling In 58
   Recipe 3 – Simple Invocation 60
   Recipe 4 – Elegant Invocation 64
   Recipe 5 – Invocation-Key Words – Very simple example 72
   Recipe 6 – Chart – Directions & Attributes 76

vii

5. JOURNEY WORK 81
    Three Worlds by *Penelope* (Illustration) 82
    Recipe 7 – Measure the Strength of Your Intention..................... 86
    Ritual 4   Elegant – Journey to the Lower World 88
    Ritual 5   Simple – Journey to the Lower World 94
    Ritual 6   Simple – Journey to the Upper World 96
    Ritual 7   Journey To The Middle World 97

6. CHAKRAS 101
    Chakras by *Penelope* (Illustration)..102
    Introduction to Lower 3 Chakras 107
        1st – Root; 2nd – Sacral; 3rd – Solar Plexus 107
    1st – Root: Location & Attributes 109
    2nd – Sacral: Location & Attributes..110
    3rd – Solar Plexus: Location & Attributes 111
    Introduction to Heart Chakra (The Bridge) 112
    4th – Heart: Location & Attributes 113
    Introduction to Upper 3 Chakras..114
        5th – Throat; 6th – Third Eye; 7th – Crown........................ 114
    5th – Throat: Location & Attributes 115
    6th – Third Eye: Location & Attributes 116
    7th – Crown: Location & Attributes..117
    Chakra Attributes and Power Animals – Key Words 118
    Chakra Attributes and Power Animals – Summary........................121
    Chakra Attributes and Power Animals – Chart 126

7. RITUALS & CEREMONIES 131
    Celebrate by *Penelope* (Illustration)..132
    Recipe 8 – Key Points in Creating Ritual 136
    Ritual 8   Ritual of Blessings of/for Prosperity 138
    Recipe 9 – Prayer Stick 140
    Energy Clearing / Removing Blocks 141
    Ritual 9   Energy Clearing for a Person...................................144
    Ritual 10 Clearing the Energy of a Building or Business 148
    Ritual 11 House Blessing...150

8. BREATHING & MEDITATION 155
    Meditation 156
    Brain Wave Activity During Meditation 157
    Recipe 10 – For Living a Full & Blessed Life 159
    Breathing 163
    Breathe by *Penelope* (Illustration) 164
    Recipe 11 – Complete Breathing 165
    Recipe 12 – Circular Breathing 166
    Recipe 13 – Rhythmic Breathing 170
    Recipe 14 – Cleansing Breath 172
    Meditation by *Penelope (Illustration)* 175
    Recipe 15 – Simple Meditation for Relaxation and Stress Release ... 177
    Recipe 16 – Unified Chakra – Light Body Meditation 182

9. THE BEGINNING 190
Quick Guide 191
Final Words: 193
Glossary 196

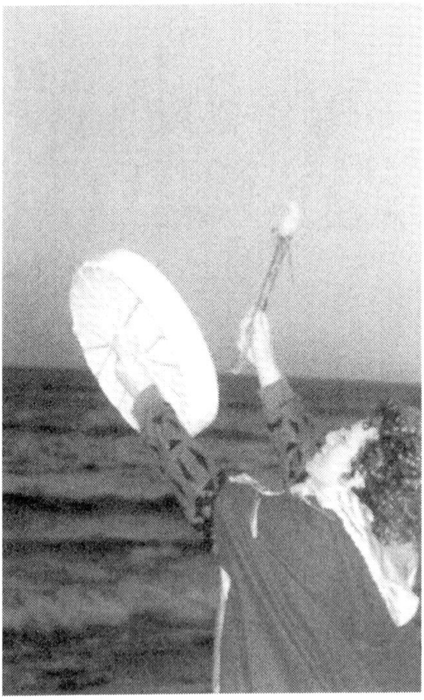

Prologue

Welcome to our book, *A SHAMANIC WAY: Rituals, Rattles, and Recipes for Awakening Your Inner Spirit*. We would love for you to have an optimum experience using this Shamanic practice guide developed with our own experiences and mistakes over our years of practice.

WHAT IS A SHAMAN??

It is known that a Shaman is a person who has the ability to travel to the Spiritual World at will, becoming a bridge or a messenger between the physical world and the Spiritual World.

HOW DOES THIS HELP??

One of the primary guiding principals for the Shaman is that any problem, illness, or disharmony in the physical world relates directly to the soul. Therefore, problems of the soul can be treated in the Spiritual World. The healing that takes place in the Spiritual World is reflected in the physical world. The role of the Shaman is to bring back pertinent information to the client, work in the Spiritual World to heal a person's soul, and thus assist healing on the physical, energetic, spiritual, emotional, and mental levels.

WHAT IS THE ROLE OF THE SHAMAN IN THE MODERN WORLD??

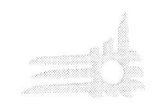

In this millennium a Shaman is not usually the spiritual leader of their community as it was in ancient time. A modern Shaman works on behalf of her/himself, family, pets, household, friends, community, and ultimately globally. This means living life in A Shamanic Way is a healing practice entered into with purity of intention, without ego aggrandizing, and without expectations of recognition. In some circles the term "I am a Shaman" is frowned upon. This is strictly a personal choice in the topic of "labeling".

The *first* thing to tell you is that living life in A Shamanic Way is that of NOTICING, or to be aware. In noticing you will find that you are more easily accessing "the NOW" or the "PRESENT". You may have heard the expression "the Present is a Present because that is all there is, the here and now." However, without noticing or being aware of the world around you, you will miss it as you live your life ruminating over the past or in worry about the future. The Shaman is a person who lives in conscious awareness of the NOW or the Present. Our book will teach you how to do just that.

How to use this book? The *second* thing we would like to share with you is that *the information in this book is not the end all, be all to learning A Shamanic Way.* We encourage your independent investigation of the truth as it is for you personally. The information we are sharing is what works for us and is intended as simply a guide or a jump off point for you to develop your own style and techniques. In our book you will find recipes, rituals, and lessons that illustrate the salient points we are trying to impart.

The *third* thing we need to share is living life in A Shamanic Way requires a high level of ethics and integrity. A Shamanic Way of life is one of working with energy which has no boundaries. As such it is a healing work. Working with energy in A Shamanic Way for yourself is a very personal endeavor. Once mastered the urge to help others in A Shamanic Way may tend to move you into the realm of being a Shamanic Healer. Despite any awakened yearnings to help others in this Way, permission must always be asked and granted prior to working with another's energy in any way.

You will notice as you develop in A Shamanic Way your intuition or psychic ability will increase. You may sense things about a person and want to be helpful. This is well and fine but take care in how you phrase your observation. No one wants to believe they can be read like an open book and a well intentioned phrase such as: "I sense you are unsettled", may cause your friend to feel unsafe with you. Phrasing such as "How are you?" or "What's going on with you nowadays?" allows that person to retain their privacy if they should not care to share with you what is going on. Your desire to help is noble but the person to be helped is the priority.

Maintaining ethical integrity is a critical component of living life in A Shamanic Way and we cannot stress its importance enough. A simple and perhaps silly example could be: What if you have a cold and you want to have the cold because you want an excuse to skip work or school? Someone does energetic healing on you without your permission and all of a sudden you no longer have a legitimate excuse to ditch school or work. Another perhaps more serious example could be: Suppose you are dating someone and have strong feelings for that person and your parent or friend does not believe you are on the right path. They perform energetic healing or ceremony to break your bond with that person and it is effective. Your personal business is only your business, not the business of a well intentioned person with some training in energy work. As you can see by these random examples maintaining high integrity and ethical standards is very much a responsibility of a person living life in A Shamanic Way.

We wanted to share with you our different backgrounds as Shamanic practioners. The techniques that we use are very similar with the exception of a few cultural differences and are noted throughout our book. These similarities illustrate the cohesive component of Shamanism and its practice around the world. Whether it is here in the United States as it is being rediscovered beyond the practice of the indigenous tribes, or in México and elsewhere in the world where it has remained a cultural practice throughout the ages.

We set up the format of our book to include Journaling pages at the end of each chapter. We encourage you to use them and date them so you are able to track your progress as you develop your Shamanic life. You may even want to note where it was you made your journal entry. As you work your way through our book you will find that journaling is a key component to your growth in Shamanic practice.

Your use of our book and its content will lead you into an opportunity to develop your life in A Shamanic Way. You may simply take this information in as food for thought or as a mental exercise, or you may take this information, fine tune it for your own use and notice the evolution of living your life in A Shamanic Way. Your objective is up to you and yours alone.

Chapter 1

TO BEGIN WITH

- Journal Pages
- What is Shamanism and "A Shamanic Way"?
- What is Shamanic Healing, Soul Retrieval, Extraction, Cord Cutting?
- Journal Pages

*"If thou but settest foot on this Path,
thou shalt see it everywhere…"*

Hermes Trismegistus

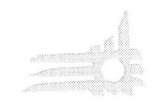

A Shaman's World

Chapter 1
TO BEGIN WITH

Welcome to <u>A SHAMANIC WAY: Rituals, Rattles, and Recipes for Awakening Your Inner Spirit</u>. Our intention in providing you with this book is to give you an overall guide for learning Shamanic Ways. This is not intended as an anthropological work documenting Shaman history through the ages and around the world, nor is it intended as the ONLY way for you to acquire Shamanic skills. A Shamanic Way is much more involved than what is offered here, however this book will provide you with basic skills to start developing your life in A Shamanic Way.

Like anything, as you learn, as you experience, you will grow. Your practice will become more and more personalized as you find what works for you.

Shamanism is an almost timeless practice, those in the know believe it to be as much as 40,000 years ancient, and is used primarily for healing purposes. Culturally Shamanic traditions are interwoven with ritual and ceremony. Core shamanism is not ritually based but similarities of approach can be found on every continent. Essentially core shamanism is the ability to move between states of consciousness at will and access both ordinary reality as we all do everyday and non-ordinary reality, a place of infinite knowledge, wisdom, and energy. The rituals, ceremonies, and Sacred Tools used are culturally specific to the person performing the Shamanic practice. This includes you. You will find the right tools, the right methods, and right songs that work for you as you grow in your knowledge and experience. A Power song may come to you, a smudging song may come to you. These are not necessarily songs with words but may simply be sounds you vocalize.

Shamanic thought is that all things both animate objects and inanimate objects, have Spirit and have energy, and that everything is connected through that Spirit and energy. In other words, the energy of a rock is as potent as the energy of a person. There are ***four (4) kingdoms***; plant, mineral, animal, and human. All of these kingdoms manifest energies that interconnect and affect our life on a daily basis.

Developing relationships with the plant, mineral, and animal kingdoms is a key component of developing one's Shamanic abilities and as important as our relationships with our fellow humans. These relationships are forged in both ordinary reality and in non-ordinary reality (as in the Spirit world). A Shamanic Way is also integrated in relationship with the ***four (4) elements*** of fire, earth, air, and water. With practice your Shamanic abilities will connect you with a tangible thread to the four kingdoms and the four elements. A recipe is included for you to "feel" each kingdom and how everything is connected by energy.

<u>*A SHAMANIC WAY*: Rituals, Rattles, and Recipes for Awakening Your Inner Spirit</u> is an introduction to Shamanism that combines both core Shamanism and ritual or ceremony. It is a demonstration for you to build upon speeding up your own experience and development of Shamanic practice in your everyday life and in living life in A Shamanic way.

It is said that a Shaman becomes a Shaman in one of three ways. The *first* is to be born into a line of Shamans, carrying on a tradition that is centuries old within a specific culture. This of course is, with some exceptions, not really a viable option in Western culture. The *second* way is to be trained by a Shaman after receiving a calling; a dream, a traumatic experience, or a near-death experience. This also is not a common occurrence in Western culture. However, there is a third way, accessible to all. Because of the inquisitive nature about Shamanism and Spiritual issues of many in Western culture a wide variety of books approaching these subjects have been written. <u>*A SHAMANIC WAY*: Rituals, Rattles, and Recipes for Awakening Your Inner Spirit</u> is yet another approach. It is designed and written as an experiential guide.

This book is influenced by Native American traditions of ceremony and ritual and includes information on basic energy work. This reflects the training, work, and experience of the author.

NOTE: Please *Remember* that our book and the information, recipes, and rituals offered are simply guidelines. There is NO RIGHT WAY OR WRONG WAY. The terms we used such as "required", "should" or "must" are the result of what works for us. Your job, should you choose, is to discover what works specifically for you. Living life in A Shamanic Way is a very personal undertaking.

Journal Page

Journal Page

Journal Page

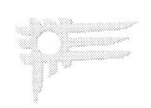

What is Shamanism and 'A Shamanic Way'?

If you consider that Shamanism is simply _knowledge and the understanding that everything has Spirit, everything is energy, and everything is interconnected_, the concept is easy to grasp

A Shamanic Way

The shamanic process is an ancient method of honoring the energy of Spirit within us and around us. Shamanic healing works on the energetic body, which affects the physical, mental, emotional, and spiritual bodies. This practice is indigenous to the entire planet and to every culture. You might say this was humanity's original belief system for both healing and religion. It predates all current religions and sciences by tens of thousands of years.

In America people equate Shamanism with Native American customs and culture. In fact that culture and those customs are specific to the Native Americans whereas core shamanism is the nearly universal principles and practices of shamanism and not connected to any specific cultural group or perspective. For instance a core shamanic ritual, such as "Soul Retrieval", will be performed similarly on any continent globally, but the music, herbs or plants used, and the language will be different and culturally specific. It is only in the Western cultures that these age-old practices and rituals have been ignored or lost. Fortunately these are now finding their way back into the healing arts.

Utilizing ancient methods a Shamanic healer or practitioner <u>accesses the Spirit world or "non-ordinary reality" by a process called a "journey". This is a type of altered state or a "shamanic state of consciousness." It may also be known as a deep meditation for accessing the subconscious mind.</u> In Shamanic work typically this is achieved by means of drumming, rattling or other repetitive sound. <u>In this altered state, Spirit can provide information through power animals, spirit guides, angels and other helpful entities. The Shamanic practitioner literally becomes that pure and hollow vessel, a conduit, through which Spirit can do its healing work.</u>

The classic shamanic journey is one of the most visionary methods used by humankind to explore the hidden universe otherwise known mainly through myth and dream. Shamanic journeying is typically facilitated by non-drug techniques such as drumming and rattling. These and other methods are used to access a Shamanic state of consciousness and for awakening dormant spiritual abilities, including connections with the Spirit world and with nature.

<u>*A SHAMANIC WAY:* Rituals, Rattles, and Recipes for Awakening Your Inner Spirit</u> will teach you how to approach your life in A Shamanic Way. In so doing you will eliminate blocks, identify your path and strategy for achievement, heal old wounds allowing you to approach your life from a different perspective, validate your worthiness, and change your patterns allowing access to the magic of your life.

NOTE: Other journey methods include a wide variety of instruments depending on the culture, psychotropic drugs and plants, undergoing extreme physical stress, and fasting. We do not recommend the use of drugs or plants. These shortcuts often have negative consequences and/or side effects. If drugs or plant psychotropics are used a profound experience may be had, however there may be lingering doubt over the veracity of the experience. Was it real or the drug?

Fasting is really not a healthy way to achieve the Shamanic state of consciousness either. Going without food and water for an extended period of time can easily be counter productive to your health. Additionally, developing your ability to journey in this moment is the ultimate goal. If you need to access information quickly you do not want to be waiting days until your fast creates a psychotropic effect.

Shamanic Healing, Soul Retrieval, Extraction and Cord Cutting

There is a time and a place for the many and varied healing arts available. Shamanic belief holds that a person has five (5) bodies, the physical, mental, emotional, energetic, and spiritual. Often times the healing of the energetic body is required to finally heal that old injury, to lift the weight of the world off our shoulders, or to validate our worthiness.

Shamanic healing works on the energetic body, which in turn affects the physical, mental, emotional, and spiritual bodies. It includes extraction of negative or counter productive energies, cord cutting of energy ties to people or things that no longer serve our higher purpose, chakra balancing and opening energy channels, energy grid realignment and activation.

What if dedicated effort has not seemed to manifest the life changes you desire?

What if your illness, physical discomfort, or injury just will not respond to medical care?

What if you feel blocked each time you attempt to move forward or change direction in your life?

What if despite a sense of overall happiness and contentment there is still something not quite right?

Assisting people in their individual journey back to a whole, healthy, abundant, and happy life is the core of Shamanic healing. Helping people heal themselves often includes the performance of the ritual known as a Soul Retrieval.

Soul Retrieval is but one component of the many facets of care of the soul.

Soul Retrieval

The Soul Retrieval ritual is an integral part of Shamanic healing.

Through trauma, illness, or injury a person may lose a piece of that vital life force we call the soul. This loss is a defense mechanism of the soul. The pain would be even greater if the person stayed whole during the trauma. In Shamanic belief this part goes into another reality or the Spirit world, often waiting for the call to come back. In modern psychology this fragmentation is known as disassociation, there is acceptance and an acknowledgment of the loss, but there is no effort made to bring the pieces back. The ritual the Shamanic healer performs to bring these pieces back and restore them to the person is known as Soul Retrieval.

Through the ritual of Soul Retrieval a person will experience a sense of wholeness and integration of self. **Remembering** the trauma associated with the original soul loss is not required in Shamanic healing. Only the reintegration and the honoring of the returning soul pieces is necessary for the healing process. In Shamanic healing the concern is to bring back lost Soul pieces and move forward. **Remembering** is not required for healing.

The Soul Retrieval process includes a Shamanic journey into non-ordinary reality. The Shamanic healer "journeys" and lost soul pieces that want to come back and be helpful are invited to "return home" to the person being healed. Upon return to ordinary reality the Shaman blows the returning soul pieces back into the person via Spiritual doors, usually the heart and into the top of the head. Then the Shamanic healer will typically seal all the Spiritual doors to anchor the returned soul parts in the recipients mental, spiritual, energetic, emotional, and physical bodies.

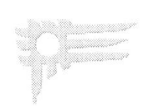

When the ritual is completed the recipient's work begins. Actively integrating, processing, and welcoming back those returned soul pieces facilitates healing into the whole, healthy, abundant, and happy person we were created to be.

Extraction and Cord Cutting

The word 'extraction' is the terminology used and does not imply a cutting open. It is simply a process done through a Shamanic journey to remove any unhelpful energy that enters the emptiness resulting from soul loss. This unhelpful or negative energy can create an environment that leads to disease: physical, emotional, and/or mental. In addition, the negative energy of depression, anger, fear, anxiety, hatred, and chronic levels of unhappiness are often the result of exposure to our society and daily life. Just living life we can experience soul loss on a daily basis allowing these negative energies to take up residence in our bodies. Extracting this negative energy restores the soul to its original divinity bringing us to a healthy, happy, abundant, and whole state of being.

The following is an example of when an extraction and Soul Retrieval needs to be performed.

A client of ours, Amy, was riding her bicycle and fell severely injuring her leg. Her injury required a four hour surgery to fix it and eighteen months of recovery. She was devastated not just because she had incredible pain, and found herself in a walker – once she could move her leg at all – but worried constantly about how she would take care of herself financially as she was a single person, living alone, with no insurance. Her trauma and worry caused significant soul loss. Her leg healed and she fell again in the same way. However, she did not injure herself, thank goodness, but her body went into shock because it **Remembered** the trauma of the original injury.

She found herself laying flat on her back, with no one around, and her body was shaking and a cold sweat had broken out all over her body. She knew she had not really hurt herself again, but experienced nausea, feeling faint, and shaking. She came to us and we performed an extraction and Soul Retrieval. Amy experienced significant soul loss when she had her initial bike accident and injury. We removed the negative memory/energy held in her body that had entered the gap left in her energy field due to her soul loss and her lost soul parts were invited to return.

As we go through our life and our experiences we become energetically connected to people, places, and things. In Shamanic belief this connection extends to people, places, and things in non-ordinary reality as well as the here and now. During a Shamanic state of consciousness the practitioner can see the cords and webs making those connections. Cutting and clearing away the cords that are unhelpful and binding in detrimental ways allows the person to change patterns and move forward in life.

A common example of the need for cutting cords is divorce. The entanglement of the two people involved can appear to the Shamanic practitioner as just that. A tangle of thick cords or a web or cocoon imprisoning them. Cutting these cords and web like substances frees the individuals to move forward in their lives in a healthy way.

Journal Page

Journal Page

Chapter 2
SACRED TOOLS

- **Sacred Smoke** – Smudging
- **Ritual 1** – Smudging
- **Medicine Plants**
- Journal Pages
- **Sacred Tools**
- **Creating Sacred Space**
- Journal Pages

Sacred herbs sprinkled begin to glow
Sacred fragrant smoke spirals upward
Sacred smoke carries prayers to Spirit above
Sacred drums
Sacred rattles
Sacred flutes
Sacred music to Spirit above
Sacred rocks
Sacred feathers
Sacred space hasten prayers to Spirit above

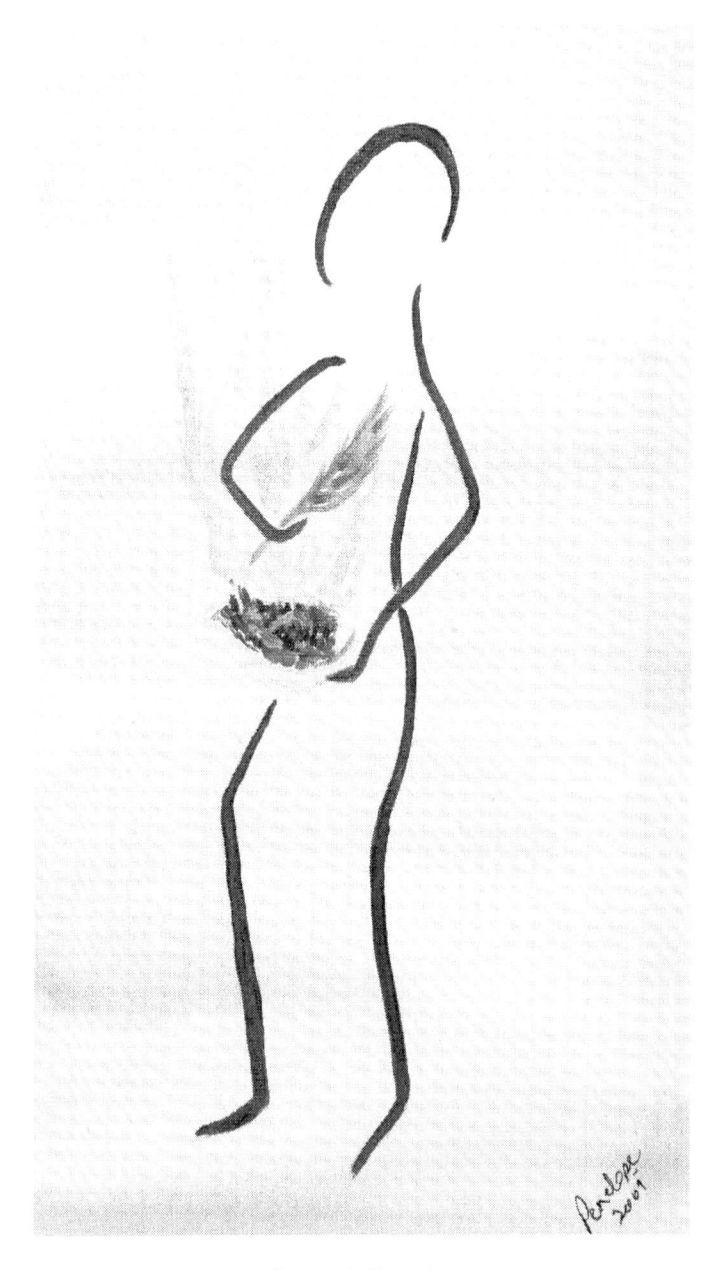

Sacred Smoke

Chapter 2
SACRED SMOKE
The Ancient Ritual of Smudging

The ritual of smudging is ancient and followed by many traditions and cultures. This includes the Christian traditions of burning incense in a chalice such as in Catholic and Orthodox followings.

Smudging is the act of cleansing the energetic body of any negative energy that may have been picked up during the course of the day. Typically any Shamanic work begins with smudging with Sacred Smoke. Depending on the work you are performing you may end your ritual with smudging as well.

Sacred smoke is used to cleanse the energetic field of a person, a building, a space, or pretty much anything as well as ceremonial/ritual tools such as drum, rattle, and feathers. It is also used to carry prayers and intention to Spirit or God. The herbs used are typically sage, sweet grass, cedar or a combination depending on what is available geographically. Obviously, purchased herbs do not hold that limitation.

The herbs are burned as loose leaves or even branches or in tied bundles or braids. Lighting may be done with a flame, placed on an open fire or upon hot rocks, such as in a sweat lodge, or with self-igniting charcoal. In the case of cedar, tobacco, copal or other resin rich substances dense with oil, ignition is not self-sustained. Self-igniting charcoal or open flame or hot rocks are required to maintain its ignition.

Pay attention to your reaction to the smoke as for some there may be an adverse reaction. Be mindful of the amount of smoke you generate. A little goes a long way. Your intention is the critical key for creating sacred smoke.

RITUAL 1
Smudging

1. Align yourself with the medicine of the herbs you will use for smudging.

NOTE: Use the method of aligning with energy of the plant kingdom as described in Chapter 1, Recipe 1 "Connecting to Energy".

2. Close your eyes.
3. Take three (3) slow deep breaths.
4. Connect with the spirit of the herb medicine.
5. Open your eyes.
6. Ignite your herbs in a receptacle such as a shell or dish if you are using loose herbs.

NOTE: If you use a smudge stick or braid be aware that embers will fall as it burns through.

If you are utilizing self-igniting charcoal place your receptacle on a surface that will not be adversely affected by the heat of your shell or dish. Break off small pieces of the self-igniting charcoal from the brick for using just what you need. Light just a corner of the piece and as it is self-igniting its ignition will expand.

Self-igniting charcoal gets exceedingly hot. An alternative is to put a layer of sand or soil in the receptacle and place the charcoal on top of that.

It is not appropriate to blow on the smudge source to enhance ignition as this is considered disrespectful and taints the smoke. Sacred Smoke is considered a living entity and blowing on it is really not acceptable any more than if you were to blow your breath into your friends face.

7. Once the herbs or resin has been lit and is smoking, set your intention for cleansing the energetic body and the

smoke is fanned with a feather, a branch, or your hand over the person to be smudged.

NOTE: Fanning is actually a brushing or stroking motion of the smoke away from the source towards the person's heart, this includes you if you are smudging yourself. Then move the smoke in the same brushing type manner over the head, down the torso, and over and under outspread arms – from shoulder to hand and fingers, down the legs and behind the back. Feel the energy of the smoke enter your heart and radiate throughout your body. Any tools to be used in your ritual are also purified in this manner.

You may feel inclined to sing a song during the smudging ritual, it may have words, it may simply have sounds or tones. It does not matter, this can become your smudging song.

If you are smudging someone be sure to smudge yourself first – to purify your efforts, then smudge your client, then smudge yourself again to clear any energy that you may have picked up from your client.

8. Offer Sacred Smoke to the cardinal directions by facing in those directions: North, East, South, and West. Then honor the four spiritual directions: Above, Below, Within, and Around.

NOTE: The attributes of the directions are explained in Chapter 4 "Calling in the Directions". Honoring the directions in this manner the smoke is fanned by the hand or a feather, or simply held up towards the direction.

Mexican smudging is often done with a large quantity of blended herbs being burned at one time and the person either steps across the burning herbs and through the smoke or stands above the smoke.

Whether you gather your smudging herbs or buy them it is important to speak to them from your heart. Shamanic tradition recognizes that everything has energy, has Spirit, and is interconnected with everything else. Showing respect for Plant Energy includes asking their permission to be picked and thanking them for partnering with you in your smudging ritual or other work.

If your medicine herb Plant Energy is the store bought type take a minute to connect with the herbs you select and feel their energy. Notice if they were harvested with sacred intention. You will feel a difference and eventually find the appropriate resource for you. You may order your Sacred plants from a nursery and establish your own Spirit garden. Once again inviting your selected plant to partner with you is essential in honoring their plant energy and maintaining its "aliveness".

There are many herbs used in smudging with different purposes. The most common are: Sage, Cedar, Cypress, Juniper, and Sweet Grass. These are typically used for purification and in creating Sacred space.

Other medicine plants for smudging:

- California Bay is used to protect against colds and flu and is typically burned in the fall of the year.
- Epazote or Mexican Tea is helpful in establishing personal boundaries.
- Fennel is used to repeal evil energies and originated during the middle ages in Europe.
- Lemon Grass is used to connect with the feminine especially Mother Earth.
- Mint is used for cleansing and uplifting of Spirit.
- Mugwort is used for healing, divination, and dreaming. It is unsafe during pregnancy.

- Mullein is helpful in healing traumas, protection in new endeavors, and for grounding and calming.
- Pine, Fir, Hemlock, and Spruce are conifers that purify and cleanse.
- Resin, Balsam, Copal, Gum, and other various types of Sap are used to affirm our connection to the Creator. Trees from which resins come are grounded in Mother Earth and reach to Father Sky. Resin smudge embodies the four elements: water and earth, and fire is introduced which then produces smoke (air).
- Sweet Grass attracts positive energies.
- Tobacco stimulates wisdom and carries prayers to Spirit or God, and provides protection.
- Uva Ursi is calming and grounding. It is often mixed with tobacco for the Sacred Pipe Ceremony.
- Yerba Santa is excellent for personal encouragement or courage, and to protect the Sacredness within you.

Journal Page

Journal Page

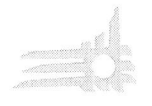

Sacred Space-Sacred Tools

Sacred Shamanic Tools

Shamanic work involves a variety of tools. These are referred to as Sacred Medicine and are dedicated to Shamanic work. As such they are blessed each and every time they are employed. Sacred tools should be cleansed after each use to maintain the purity of your intention upon use. These tools can be something as simple as a rock or crystal to something very elaborate and elegant such as a dedicated sacred space in which to do your Shamanic work. Typically the Sacred tools are made of natural elements: wood, feathers, shell, skins, rock, etc. This is not a given and it is a very individualistic and personal decision what you use, what resonates for you.

Musical instruments are frequently dedicated to Shamanic work. Drums, rattles, flutes, didgeridoos, thumb harps, Tibetan singing bowls, cymbals, bells, dried gourds, really any sound making instrument. It can be as simple as two sticks that you tap together, or two rocks. It could even be something you create. The drum is generally an integral part of Shamanic work as it is used to facilitate the "journey" of the Shamanic practitioner.

Rocks, crystals, shells, and bones are often part of the Sacred Tool Kit. Fabric, ribbons, beads, skins, mirrors, feathers, and really anything that enhances your practice or decorates your Sacred Space are part of your tools.

Methods for Cleansing Sacred Tools

- Smudging your tools with Sacred Smoke is something that should be done before and after each use.
- Leave your tools in direct sunlight for two hours. Be careful however as the UV rays tend to deteriorate most materials with the exception of rocks and crystals.

- Your rocks and stones can also be cleansed in running water, preferably from a natural source such as rainwater, a creek, river, or the ocean. However, faucet water can be used if need be.
- As always intention is everything, so blessing your tools before and after each use is very important. You are essentially thanking them for their help. **Remember** they are infused with Spirit.

Creating a Dedicated Sacred Space

Again this is a very individualistic and personal preference.
(See Chapter 4, "Calling in the Directions".)

Your resonance with a specific direction/s will give you important information regarding:

- The orientation of your body position.
- Which direction your head is in.
- Which direction your feet are pointing.
- The positioning of your Sacred tools: rocks, crystals, feathers, candles, etc.
- The position of your altar space; an integral part of your Sacred Space.
- The type of material you will use for lying upon: a blanket, piece of fabric, pillows, etc.

Your altar space holds the items that are close to your heart, it also holds items that pertain to a specific Shamanic task, whatever that may be for you. The altar space should be kept clear of clutter and maintained in terms of dusting and blessing with Sacred Smoke. It may contain a mirror in which you can see your Sacred Self when you engage your altar. Your Sacred Space can be decorated to enhance its special feel. Using feathers, ribbons, lace, skins, candles, etc., the decorating is again, very personal.

As you can see creating your Sacred Shamanic Tool Kit or "medicine bag" is extremely personal and individualized. If you have a question about something you are contemplating using in your Shamanic work we suggest you "journey" on it and see what Spirit guides you to do.
(See Chapter 5, "Journey Work".)

***Remember you can trust that small inner voice
and with practice trust will grow.***

Journal Page

Journal Page

Journal Page

Chapter 3

CREATING SACRED CIRCLE

- **Recipe 1 – Sacred Circle** – Simple Example
- **Recipe 2 – Sacred Circle** – Elegant Example
- Journal Pages

Sacred circle created with purity of intention
Sacred circle host of protection and strength
Sacred circle focus our energy
Sacred circle energize us in your wisdom
Sacred circle thank you for being

Sacred Circle

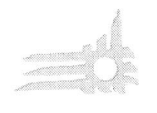

Chapter 3
CREATING SACRED CIRCLE

As in anything done in A Shamanic Way, either a simple or elegant approach will work equally well because INTENTION is everything. It really depends on what works best for you. <u>A Sacred Circle delineates a Sacred Space within which your ritual or ceremony is performed.</u> This is established in as many ways as there is imaginative and creative thought.

We provide a simple approach and an elegant approach from which you can use as a jump off point to create your own special Sacred Circle. You will find that your creation of Sacred Space will be unique to the ritual or ceremony you intend to perform.

In Native American tradition a Sacred Circle is created in a clockwise direction. This is the direction for bringing in new energy. A gap or door is left in one of the cardinal directions. It is typically in the east, as the east is new beginnings, but it can be in whatever direction Spirit guides you to leave open. It is through that door that you will step with your Sacred Tools. You will close it when you have entered. You will open your door when your ritual is completed and the directions have been thanked. It is important to remove the Sacred Circle in the opposite direction it was created in; in this case, a counter clockwise direction. Again this is a method of thanksgiving for the opportunity to work in Sacred Space. Clockwise brings in energy and counter clockwise releases the energy.

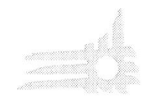

NOTE: If you are working in a public space such as a beach or in the forest you will want to remove any indication of your Sacred Circle such as dispersing the objects used to delineate the Circle, or brushing away your drawing in the sand or dirt of the Circle. This action, too, should be performed in a reverent and respectful manner in the appropriate direction.

Please *Remember* that our book and the information, recipes, and rituals offered are simply guidelines. There is NO RIGHT WAY OR WRONG WAY. The terms we used such as "required", "should" or "must" are the result of what works for us. Your job, should you choose, is to discover what works specifically for you. Living life in A Shamanic Way is a very personal undertaking.

RECIPE 1:

SIMPLE SACRED CIRCLE

1. Find a quiet space without interruptions in which to create your Sacred Circle.
2. Stand comfortably within your dedicated space (shoes on or off is optional and up to you).
3. Close your eyes.
4. Breathe 3 times very slowly and deeply from your abdomen.
5. Bring your hands in front of your chest, palms facing each other and 7 inches apart.
6. Breathe deeply again and feel the energy coming from Mother Earth into your feet, moving up your body until the energy reaches your hands.
7. Move your hands slowly, as though massaging a ball, until your feel something such as a tickling, warmth, coldness, or any other sensation (this is the energy).
8. Move your hands closer together and feel the difference.
9. Separate your hands a little bit and feel the difference.
10. Notice how we have this energy; feel it, try to smell it, hear it, taste it, use all your senses.
11. Open your eyes.

12. Walk around the room or space in a clockwise direction bringing in the energy while smudging with Sacred Smoke and holding your intention of creating Sacred Space. Walk around three (3) times.

13. You may sing, rattle or drum while walking in a reverent clockwise direction (this is up to you).

14. Upon creation of your Sacred Space the directions are "called in" as described in Chapter Four "Calling In the Directions".

NOTE: In the case of a Simple Sacred Circle you need not leave a door as described in the Elegant Sacred Circle process as you are already within your Sacred Space.

15. Upon completion of your ritual or ceremony; give thanks and walk in a counterclockwise direction releasing the energy to open your Sacred Space. Walk around three (3) times.

RECIPE 2:

ELEGANT SACRED CIRCLE

1. Align your energy as described in the Simple Circle recipe Steps 1-11.

2. Delineate your Sacred Circle by literally creating a circle on the ground. Use natural objects or simply draw a circle in the dirt or sand. Create your Sacred Circle in a clockwise direction leaving a gap or a door at one of the four (4) cardinal directions as described earlier in this chapter's introduction.

3. Smudge yourself, anyone who is going to be within your Sacred Circle, and your Sacred Tools prior to entering your Sacred Space.

4. Enter your Sacred Circle with whatever objects, Sacred Tools, and people are to be a part of your ritual or ceremony.

5. Close your door by completing the drawing or adding additional objects to block the door.

6. Smudge your Sacred Circle by walking in a clockwise direction three (3) times bringing in the energy.

7. Call in the directions, as described in the following chapter.

8. Perform your ritual or ceremony.

9. Give a formal thank you to the powers that you invited in and to all helping entities and energies.

10. Open the door that you entered through.

11. Step out of your Sacred Space.

12. Remove your delineating objects or markers in a counterclockwise direction, releasing the energy, as described earlier.

NOTE: In the Mexican tradition the Sacred Circle can be created with herbs like pine needles, pirul (pepper tree), or a mixture of the herbs from the last chapter. Prodigiosa (mugwort), ruda (rue), perejil (parsely), albahaca (basil), rosa de castilla (rose buds).

Journal Page

Journal Page

Journal Page

Chapter 4
CALLING IN THE DIRECTIONS
INVOCATION (Calling In)

- Journal Pages
- **Ritual 2** – Simple Calling In
- **Ritual 3** – Elegant Calling In
- **Recipe 3** – Simple Invocation
- **Recipe 4** – Elegant Invocation
- **Recipe 5** – Invocation – Key Words
- **Recipe 6** – Directions and Attributes (Chart)
- Personal Direction Chart
- Journal Pages

North
East
South
West
Above
Below
Within
Around – First and Always
Come to us now for there is always room in our hearts for you.

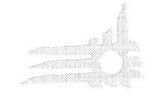

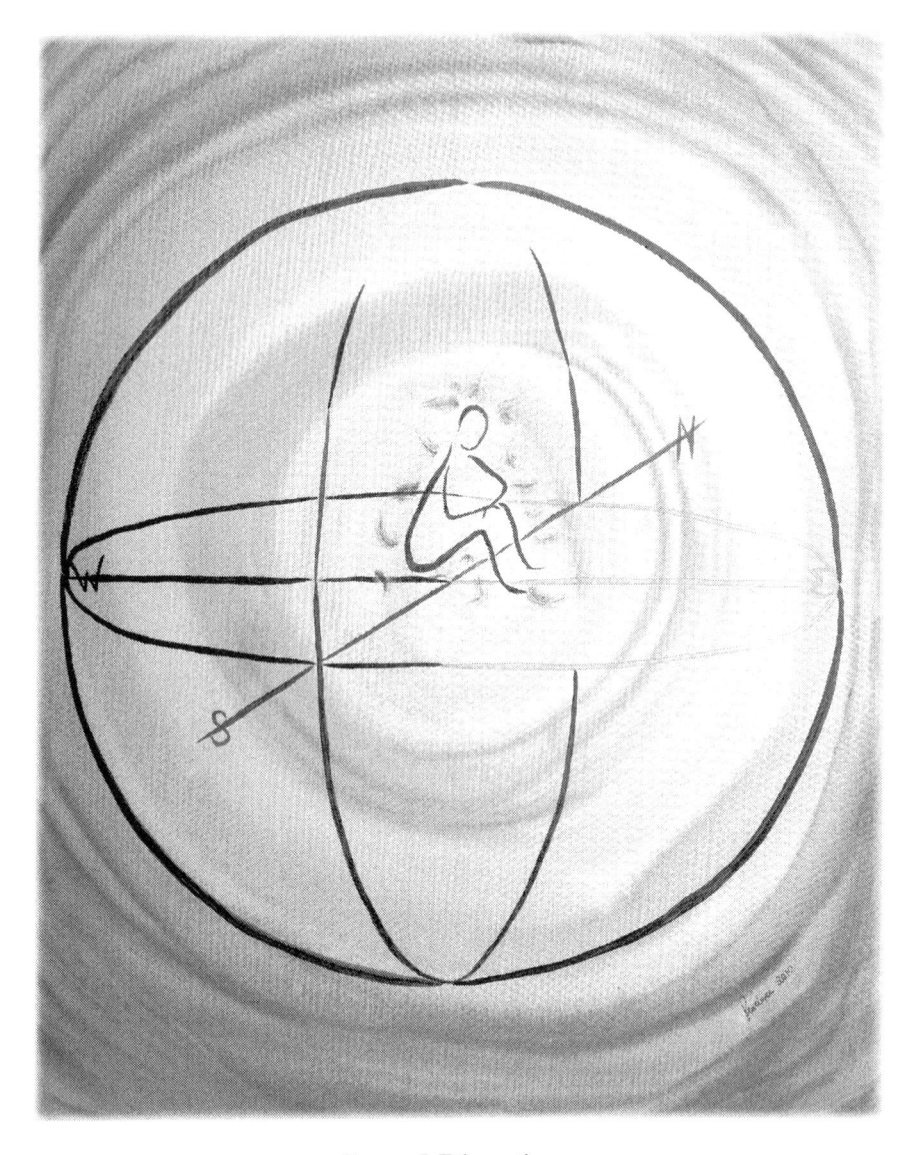

Sacred Directions

Chapter 4
"CALLING IN" THE DIRECTIONS

In Shamanic practice there are six (6) directions; the four (4) cardinal directions: North, East, South, West, and the two (2) Spirit directions; Above and Below. These have powerful energy and are invited to help create Sacred Space. The directions called are typically these six. However, energetically speaking there is actually eight. The four cardinal directions and four spirit based directions: Above, Below, Within, and Around – First and Always. The Within is also known as the heart direction.

Each ceremony, ritual, or act of intention, if performed from a Shamanic perspective, begins with calling in the directions and smudging the room, area, people, sacred tools, and altar. The invitation or "calling in" can be as simple as silent invitation with sacred smoke, to something as elaborate and elegant as using drumming, rattles, songs, and moving around to face the directions. Whether simple or elegant, this invitation is recognition and honoring the power of energies of this earth and beyond.

Pay close attention to the feelings and insights that may arise within you as you call in each direction. One direction may feel more powerful to you than the others, or not. However, typically a person will find their power direction if they pay attention as each direction is invited in. This is another reason for staying in the moment at any given moment. ***Remember*** Chapter 1, Recipe 1.

If you do feel a more prevalent power direction you may use this knowledge to build upon. For instance, direction of placement is important in the position of your body during meditation, orienting your bed in your bedroom, positioning of a dedicated Sacred Space in your home or yard, etc. Over time your power direction may change, be aware that nothing in Spirit is static or unchanging.

A Shamanic Way provides you with two examples for "calling in" the directions: A very simple ritual and an elegant ritual. Know that anything you come up with and works for you is appropriate. Again, these are simply guidelines, there is no right or wrong way.

The recipes for invocation (meaning the words for calling in the directions) are provided in both a simple version and an elegant version. We have also included a simpler version with a bullet list of each direction's attributes, and an even simpler version with just the key words for the directions. These are but samples and examples for you to create your own "calling in" of the directions. A chart for your convenience with the attributes of the directions is included. Please **Remember** that the attributes we provide may be different for you, personally, as you work with the directions, as they may be different culturally within the various indigenous peoples.

Knowing the attributes of each direction combined with guidance from the Spirit within you will allow you to create a highly specialized ritual of your own. You may find you will create more than one ritual for "calling in" of the directions based on your specific intention in that moment. There are no rules. There is no right way or wrong way. Let Spirit guide you.

Journal Page

Journal Page

Calling The Directions

RITUAL 2
Simple – Calling In

1. Create and feel your ball of energy between your hands.

(This will help you get in tune with your energy and the energy around you and will connect you to your Spirituality. Over time with practice you will be able to connect to Spirit with just two or three breaths. Intention will connect you.)

2. Smudge yourself with sacred smoke.
   (See Chapter 2, "Smudging".)

3. Sit or lay comfortably.

4. Close your eyes or use a blindfold: sleep shield, pretty scarf, or whatever works for you that will be dedicated to use during ceremony. This will then become a sacred tool.

5. Focus your mind on your breathing, notice how it will deepen and become more regular with your attention.

6. Visualize or feel yourself turning in each direction with your invitation.

7. Form your invitation in words that work for you. It is essentially a prayer for guidance, support, and acknowledgement with gratitude of power beyond you.

8. Inviting in all eight directions, six directions, or just the four cardinal directions is up to you and what feels right for you.

9. Once you have completed this opening for your ritual or ceremony, allow yourself to move into the content of your purpose or intention.

10. At the end of your ritual or ceremony extend your thanks to the directions for the assistance they provided. **NOTE:** Closing ceremony is equally important as Opening ceremony.
11. Simply focus your mind again on your breathing.
12. Visualize or feel yourself turning in each direction with your thanks, releasing your helping Spirits.
13. Close down your energy as described in Chapter 1, Recipe 2, "Connecting to Energy" Part IV, Steps 1-8.

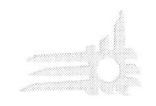

RITUAL 3
Elegant – Calling In

1. Create and feel your ball of energy between your hands.

2. Smudge yourself, the room or the space, anyone else that may be part of the ritual or ceremony, and your sacred tools. (See Chapter 2, "Smudging".)

3. Your sacred tools: drum, rattle, feathers, stones, etc. may be set up around your space to delineate your Sacred Space. <u>Pay attention to the little voice in your head that is Spirit. It will tell you the placement of which objects.</u>

4. When calling in the directions in this elegant way move around your space to face in the direction you are calling in. Use a drum, rattle, a didgeridoo, or songs. You need to create Sacred Space in a way that works for you. The attributes of the directions may be spoken aloud (see the following examples) or simply with intention. The ritual tends to FEEL more powerful if spoken aloud. However, KNOW that your INTENTION IS EVERYTHING, therefore silent invitation and acknowledgement works equally well. Again, it is what you are comfortable with or LED to do by Spirit.

5. Part of the "calling in" after your drumming or rattling you may whistle to further attract the attention of the Spirit of that direction.

6. Speak or think the attributes of each direction in your invitation.

7. Move into the content of your ritual or ceremony after the directions have been invited in.

8. At the end of your ritual or ceremony acknowledge the directions with thanks. This may be done elegantly by standing and facing in each direction as you did during the calling in or simply silently with intention.

9. Close down your energy as described in Chapter 1, Recipe 2, Part IV, Steps 1-8.

NOTE: Try calling in the directions in different places: beach, mountains, home, forest, etc. and feel the difference. ***Remember*** everything is energy and we are all connected. Also ***Remember*** to take note of any direction or location that particularly pulls on your attention or feels more powerful to you. This is significant information for personalizing your Shamanic experience and living life in A Shamanic Way.

"Calling in the Directions" is very personal. The following is an example starting with the North. This is simply an example. You will find the right starting point for yourself with practice. Additionally, directions are associated with many attributes including colors. The color and other attributes will vary depending on the cultural influence of the ceremony you are employing and on what works for you.

For instance, you may feel more comfortable with different words for your "Invocation" or "Invitation" such as addressing the Spirits of the directions with the term "Powers of the…" You may chose to not use the Lakota or other indigenous people's term for that direction.

Again, with practice you will discover the attributes that work for you. These attributes such as the colors or the specific words of your invocation may be different for you than for others. ***Remember*** there is no right or wrong way and do not allow anybody to tell you that what you are working with is wrong. Allow yourself to see your own colors and attributes as they are representative of your own personal Spirituality.

RECIPE 3:

> # CALLING IN THE DIRECTIONS
> ## Simple Invocation

Spirits of the **NORTH** – Waziyata – **(wah zee yah tah)**
You are the home of the Great Buffalo, symbol of strength, endurance, generosity, and ancient wisdom. Home of our elders, those who have gone on before us.
You are the elemental Earth.
You are the keepers of the material and physical world.
Your color is the green of the earth.
I pray that I live my life in gratitude and selflessness, walking with the wisdom of those who have gone before me.
Come to me now Waziyata – **(wah zee yah tah)** for there is always room for you in my heart.

Spirits of the **EAST** – Wiyohiyanpata – **(we yo he yan pa tah)**
You are the home of the Great Eagle, symbol of focused vision.
You are the elemental Air.
You are the keepers of intelligence, new beginnings, creativity, and mental clarity.
Your color is the gold of a new day.
I pray that I always live my life in illumination and clarity, and with wisdom.
Come to me now Wiyohiyanpata – **(we yo he yan pa tah)** for there is always room for you in my heart.

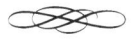

Spirits of the **SOUTH** – Itokaghata **(ee toe ka gha tah)**
You are the home of the Great Cat, symbol of active passion and the Great Snake, symbol of change.
You are the elemental Fire.
You are the keepers of passion, action, child like innocence, and the Sacred Song.
Your color is the red fire of creativity and passion.
I pray that I always live my life in harmony and balance standing strongly in my Song of Spirit, welcoming new beginnings with passion, wisdom, and childlike innocence.
Come to me now Itokaghata – **(ee toe ka gha tah)** for there is always room for you in my heart.

Spirits of the **WEST** – Wiyohpeyata – **(we yo peh yah tah)**
You are the home of the Great Bear, symbol of introspection.
You are the elemental Water.
You are the keepers of silence, emotional and spiritual illumination.
Your color is the black of the unknown.
I pray that I move gracefully into the darkness, journeying within; gaining insight and emotional and spiritual understanding with passion, clarity, and wisdom.
Come to me now Wiyohpeyata – **(we yo peh yah tah)** for there is always room for you in my heart.

Spirits of the **ABOVE** – Father Sky – Ate Mahpiya – **(ate mah pe yah)**

You are the home of Chokmah, the Father. Symbol of the Divine energy of the Creator.

You are the elemental of Fire, Water, Air and Earth. Master of the eight directions; North, East, South, West, Above, Below, Within, and Around.

You are the keepers of that energy of Spirit and the Great Star Nation.

Your color is the red of passion, the black of the unknown, and the white of purity of intention.

I pray that your Will is my will and my will is your Will guiding and supporting me at all times.

Come to me now Ate Mahpiya **(ak mah pe yah)** for there is always room for you in my heart.

Spirits of **BELOW** – Mother Earth Ina Makha – **(ee nah mah kah)**

You are the home of Binah, the Mother, symbol of the Divine womb and nurturing feminine spirit.

You are the elemental Earth.

You are the keepers of all creatures and things on the earth and below the earth and our connection to all things.

Your color is the indigo of the Universe.

I pray that I live my life as that sacred hollow bone through which Spirit can do its Divine work.

Come to me now Ina Makha **(ee nah mah kah)** for there is always room for you in my heart.

Spirits of the **WITHIN**, All My Relations – Mitakuye Oyasin – (**mi talk wee ah sin**)

You are the home of Tipereth, symbol of the Inner Voice the All Knowing consciousness.

You are the balance of the elementals of Fire, Water, Air and Earth.

You are the keeper of the Sacred Cord connecting us to the Above and to the Below.

Your color is the white of purity of thought and the red for the desire of connection.

I pray to always walk in harmony and balance with my will and God's Will being one.

Come to me now Mitakuye Oyasin (**mi talk wee ah sin**) for there is always room for you in my heart.

Spirit of **AROUND**, Great Mystery, the First and Always – Wakhan Thankan – (**walk en tonkah**)

You are the home of Kether, symbol of the beginning, the source of all existence.

You are All. You are the elementals of Fire, Water, Air and Earth

You are the keeper of Cosmic Will, the Universal Mind.

Your color is the purple for the healing power of the Universe.

I pray to always live my life with love as my point of departure and love as my point of return.

Come to me now Wakhan Thankan (**walk en tonkah**) for there is always room for you in my heart.

RECIPE 4

CALLING IN THE DIRECTIONS
Elegant Invocation

Grandfather you who stand in the **NORTH** – Waziyata **(wah zee yah tah)**

Spirit keeper of the Great White Buffalo. The place where the vital life Energy comes from. I send a voice and I humbly ask you to come to me now and help me to build a sacred hoop of power that I may walk in.

The North-home of wisdom and gratitude. I pray that I be blessed by the wisdom of the elders, those who have walked the path before me, who have traveled into the land of the white hairs. I honor that wisdom and express my gratitude for it by passing on that wisdom in a resourceful and productive way that others might benefit.

Waziyata – **(wah zee yah tah)** help me to be strong and enduring like the buffalo. With the strength of the buffalo I face into the north. Allowing the cold north winds to blow through my life bringing about the changes and the deaths that I need to go through bringing me to rebirth.

Teach me to be more like the buffalo, selfless and giving, that I learn that in giving I receive. To the point of giving up my life that the people may live and that I may be reborn.

I acknowledge that White Buffalo Calf Woman came from the North to teach me about prayer. May I always live my life as a prayer.

Come to me now Grandfather Waziyata (wah zee yah tah) for there is always room for you in my heart.

Grandfather you who stand in the **EAST** – Wiyohiyanpata **(we yo he yan pa tah)**

Spirit keeper of the Great Eagle, the place where the sun always shines, the place of new beginnings. Enter my heart and awaken your medicine of illumination, help me to see the path that lies ahead of me. I send a voice and I humbly ask you to come to me now and help me to build a sacred hoop of power that I may walk in.

The East – Home of focus, creativity, clarity, and vision. Bless me with the knowledge that comes with being able to see that which lies in front of me. Help me to see with focus, and clarity, help me to rise above and look down and see the whole picture exactly as it is.

Great Eagle teach me about vision, that I may see things in a new way and see things that I haven't seen before. Teach me about making new beginnings. Every moment can be a new beginning; a chance to start over.

Wiyohiyanpata **(we yo he yan pa tah)** thank you for the gift of vision. I pray that I have the energy and freedom to carry out the vision that I have been blessed with. Bless me with the purity and innocence of the new day and the illumination that comes with each new sunrise.

Bless me with the enlightenment which comes with the rebirth of returning to the east.

Come to me now Grandfather Wiyohiyanpata (we yo he yan pa tah) for there is always room for you in my heart.

A Shamanic Way

Grandfather you who stand in the **SOUTH** – Itokaghata **(ee toe ka gha tah)**

Spirit keeper of the Snake, a place where life comes from and life returns to. The home of my SONG. I send a voice and I humbly ask you to come to me now and help me to build a sacred hoop of power that I may walk in.

The South – Home of action, childlike innocence, and passion for life. Home of my Song. Help me to let go and step into the flow of life. Remove all fear from my heart and let my heart be filled with love that I can step into the flow of that life. Fill my heart with trust, that my trust in Spirit is strong. Teach me about innocence and awakening the child within, about having fun and spontaneity.

Help me to treat myself gently and those around me gently. Free me from labeling or judging others. Help me to participate in life and creation always adding to that creation.

Itokaghata **(ee toe ka gha tah)** remove all blocks which prevent me from growing into that which Spirit intends me to become.

Help me be open to the lessons that you present and I ask these to come to me in a loving and gentle way; always recognizing that difficulties are opportunities for growth.

I pray for healing, balance, and harmony in my life and to always live in my Song.

Come to me now Grandfather Itokaghata (ee toe ka gha tah) for there is always room for you in my heart.

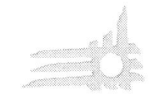

CREATING SACRED CIRCLE

Grandfather you who stand in the **WEST** – Wiyohpeyata **(we yo peh yah tah)**

Spirit keeper of the great Bear, you are the father of the four winds in the place where the spirits dwell and the home of the thunder beings. I send a voice and I humbly ask you to come to me now and help me to build a sacred hoop of power that I may walk in.

The West – Home of introspection, reflection, and looking within. Help me to look inside myself that I truly know myself and know who I am. Help me to look with courage and honesty, with humility allow me to be vulnerable in looking at myself that I know exactly who I am, and to accept all parts of me.

I pray that you Great Bear will help me to move into the darkness, into the realm of the Spirit, and that Spirit will be with me. Honoring the dream time, just like the bear going into the cave, you are the beginning of my journey into my self-discovery.

Wiyohpeyata **(we yo peh yah tah)** you are the home of the thunder beings. I honor you thunder beings for your power of life and death. You bring the life giving rains. You also hold the power of death and for that great power I honor you.

Come to me now Grandfather Wiyohpeyata (we yo peh yah tah) for there is always room for you in my heart.

A Shamanic Way

Father Sky keeper of all the things – **ABOVE**. – Ate Mahpiya **(ak mah pe yah)**

Your center is the sun, which is the direct energy of the creator. I send a voice and I humbly ask you to come to me now and help me to build a sacred hoop of power that I may walk in.

Above – Home of the life source, the masculine, that vital life force, the Divine energy. Let me be filled with this energy and allow it to radiate through me. Fill me with your energy that I may walk in the sunlight of the Spirit. Send a voice to your sister the moon a symbol of the light in the darkness, a reflection of the light of the Spirit.

Ate Mahpiya **(ak mah pe yah)** teach me about looking into the darkness, being able to see into the other side. I pray for you to come to me and teach me through my dreams and visions about that which lies below the level of my consciousness.

I acknowledge the great Star Nation, the place from where my ancestors came. I pray that I be aware of my connection with my ancestors and that I am open to their teaching and their guidance.

Help me to be open to all the universes and the universes beyond. That the universe may enter my heart, that I may now be at the center of the universe and that the universe is within me; connecting me heart, to heart, to heart.

I pray that all my actions be supported by the universe and that I always walk in harmony.

Grandfather Ate Mahpiya (ak mah pe yah) come to me now for there is always room for you in my heart.

Great Mother, Mother Earth – **BELOW** – Ina Makha **(ee nah mah kah)**

You are Mother, you are Grandmother, Unci **(Oon she)**. From you I came; to you I shall return. Awaken in my heart your earth medicine. I send a voice and I humbly ask you to come to me now and help me to build a sacred hoop of power that I may walk in.

Mother Earth – Home of nurturing, feminine spirit. Through you I come to know my connection with all living things. All things I share in spirit. It is through you grandmother I celebrate the true meaning of Mitakuye Oyasin **(me talk wee ah syn)**, all my relations.

Ina Makha **(ee nah mah kah)** I pray that I walk in right relationship with all two leggeds, four leggeds, creepy crawlers, finned ones, sacred stone people, and standing ones.

Awaken in me your divine feminine spirit. Hold me in your womb. Help me to also become a womb that my heart becomes a fertile and nurturing place for thoughts, feelings, and ideas to grow.

Mother Earth, Ina Makha (ee nah mah kah) come to me now for there is always room for you in my heart.

All my relations, the Heart – **WITHIN** – Mitakuye Oyasin **(me talk wee ah sin)**

You are the home of the inner eye, the heart of all hearts. It is through you that the cosmic connection is felt between all things and all levels. I send a voice and I humbly ask you to come to me now and help me to build a sacred hoop of power that I may walk in.

The Within – Home of all our relations. That place in all of us that knows all things. That space of our anchor, the Sacred Cord bonding us to all that is, that was, and that will be.

Mitakuye Oyasin **(mee talk wee ah sin)** I pray that I always stay connected to my inner voice; guiding me with truth and direction.

I thank you Great Spirit for the gift of inner hearing, of the listening heart, and the grace to accept the truths as they are revealed to me.

Come to me now Mitakuye Oyasin (me talk wee ah sin) for there is always room for you in my heart.

First and always have been – **AROUND** – Wakhan Thanka **(walk en tonka)**

You came before everything else. You came from the great void that created the Universe and I call you great mystery. I send a voice and I humbly ask you to come to me now and help me to build a sacred hoop of power that I may walk in.

The Universe – Home of what is all and what is nothing. The Around. Everything I see was made by you, everything I see is part of you, and you are part of everything. You are the source of all life and you gave me the gift of life. I owe you my life. I come to you in a humble and respectful way. I ask you to come to me, bless me, and guide my life.

Wakhan Thanka (**walk en tonka**) help me to pray for your will to be my will, to pray for the good of all the people.

Bless me with the sacred hoop of power that I may walk in today. I pray that you hear my prayers, receive my prayers, and that you speak to my listening heart.

Wakhan Thanka (walk en tonka) come to me now and make your presence known to me in a gentle and powerful way for there is always room in my heart for you.

RECIPE 5:

INVOCATION OF DIRECTIONS
Key Words

NORTH – Waziyata **(wah zee yah tah)**

    Earth
    Wisdom of Our Ancestors the White Hairs
    Gratitude
    Strength
    Great Buffalo

EAST – Wiyohiyanpata – **(we yo he yan pa tah)**

    Air
    Intelligence
    Illumination
    New Beginnings
    Creativity
    Clarity
    Great Eagle

SOUTH – Itokaghata **(ee toe ka gha tah)**

    Fire
    Sacred Song
    Passion
    Action
    Childlike Innocence
    Great Snake and Great Lion

WEST – Wiyohpeyata **(we yo peh yah tah)**

    Water
    Introspection
    Emotion
    Spiritual Illumination
    Thunder Beings
    Great Bear

MOTHER EARTH – Ina Makha **(ee nah mah kah)**

    Below
    Nurturing, Feminine Spirit
    Divine Womb
    All Creatures and Things Physical and Non-Physical

FATHER SKY – Ate Mahpiya (ak mah pe yah)

Above
Masculine, Life Force
Divine Energy
Cosmic intelligence
Star nation

WITHIN – All My Relations – Mitakuye Oyasin (mee talk wee ah sin)

Inner eye
Sacred Cord
Cosmic connection
The Heart Anchor to Above and Below

AROUND – Great Mystery, First and Always Wakhan Thankan (walk en tonkah)

The Ether
Everywhere and nowhere
Has always been and has never been
Everything and nothing
The All
The Universe
Cosmic Will

RECIPE 6:

DIRECTIONS & ATTRIBUTES

Direction	Native Name	Totem	Home To	Elemental	Keepers Of	Color	Gift	Prayer
North	Waziyata	Buffalo	Strength/Wisdom	Earth	Material/Physical World	Green	Selflessness	Gratitude and Wisdom
East	Wiyohiyanpata	Eagle	Illumination	Air	Intelligence, New Beginnings, Clarity	Gold	Focused Vision	Enlightenment
South	Itokaghata	Great Cat Great Snake	Passion Change	Fire	Sacred Song	Red	Passion	Creativity/Childlike Innocence
West	Wiyohpeyata	Bear	Thunder Beings	Water	Introspection, Reflection	Black	Emotional and Spiritual Illumination	Courage and Honesty
Above	Ate Mahpiya	Father Sky	Great Star Nation	Earth, Air, Fire, Water	Vital Life Force	Red, Black	Radiating Universal Energy	Sunlight of the Spirit
Below	Ina Makha	Mother Earth	Earth Medicine	Earth	Womb of Creation	Indigo	Universal Wisdom	Connection to ALL
Within	Mitakuye Oyasin	Christ/Heart Consciousness	Sacred Cord Anchoring Above and Below	Earth, Air, Fire, Water	Honored, Sacred Space of All My Relations	Red, White	Inner Guidance	Harmony and Balance
Around	Wakhan Thanka	The Source	Kether, The beginning and always	Earth, Air, Fire, Water	Cosmic Will	Purple	Healing Power of the Universe	Sacred Hoop of Power in which to Walk

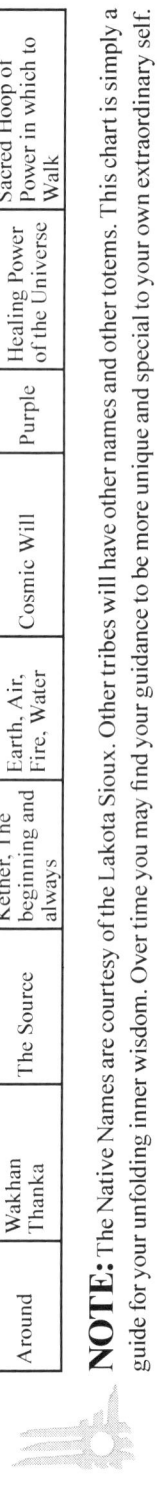

NOTE: The Native Names are courtesy of the Lakota Sioux. Other tribes will have other names and other totems. This chart is simply a guide for your unfolding inner wisdom. Over time you may find your guidance to be more unique and special to your own extraordinary self.

A Shamanic Way

CREATING SACRED CIRCLE

DIRECTIONS

Direction	Native Name	Totem	Home To	Elemental	Keepers Of	Color	Gift	Prayer
North								
East								
South								
West								
Above								
Below								
Within								
Around								

NOTE: This chart is for your personal use. With practice you may find your guidance to be more unique and special to your own magnificent self.

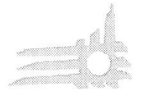

Journal Page

Journal Page

Journal Page

Chapter 5

JOURNEY WORK

- **Recipe 7** – Measure the Strength of Your Intention
- **Ritual 4** – Journey to the Lower World – Elegant
- **Ritual 5** – Journey to the Lower World – Simple
- **Ritual 6** – Journey to the Upper World – Simple
- **Ritual 7** – Journey to the Middle World – Simple
- Journal Pages

Intention is everything
In this world and the next
Bring to us the wisdom to walk with strength and courage
Always staying on the Path of Spirit's Will

Three Worlds

Chapter 5
JOURNEY WORK

Shamanism is a practice that recognizes and honors all things visible and invisible as having Spirit, energy, and being interconnected. As such they are products of, depending on your terminology: the Universe, or the Divine, or Spirit, or Creator, or God or Goddess.

This thought is not religious in nature, nor is it ruled by dogma. This is now very recently a quantum physics reality that has been simply an ancient belief system for many thousands of years, dating back to the Stone Age. The Shamanic Journey is common to all cultures across the globe and is remarkably similar in its process.

The core piece of shamanic work is the ritual called "journey". This is a process of extending one's consciousness into what is known as "non-ordinary reality" and/or "altered state". Whatever term you chose to apply it is quite simply the accessing of a different reality.

Non-ordinary reality can be divided into three locations; the upper, middle, and lower worlds. You may find in any of these locations in altered reality teachers, guides, angels, or power animals (often known as "totems"). In some cultures a Shamanic Journey is accomplished with the assistance of psychotropic plants, fasting, or undergoing extreme physical stress. These are not necessary as rhythmic repetitive drumming or rattling can provide a much SAFER vehicle for accessing the three worlds of Spirit.

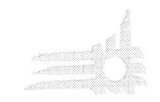

Remember your teachers, guides, angels, or power animals can appear in any of the three worlds. And for some they may transcend between two or more worlds. Once again this is very personal and these spirits are not limited in their location.

An example of the typical residents of these worlds is shown below, but this is not cast in stone.

Lower World:

A journey to the lower world may allow you to find your personal "Power Animal", may help you find your "Power Song", may allow you to recover lost "personal power", and may comfort you in providing a support system that can provide helpful knowledge. You may find with practice that you will meet power animals that function for a specific purpose in your life. Overtime you may gain a whole herd of different power animals supporting your various waking world life endeavors.

Upper World:

A journey to the upper world may allow you to access your Spirit Guide (s) or Angels. You may find your guide is one of the ascended Masters, a cosmic being, or an ancestor. With assistance from the upper world you may access lost soul parts, or find the guidance you receive is pertinent to your inner self or higher being.

Middle World:

A middle world journey is one of discovery for the everyday efforts of living life. You may find you access a parallel reality during a middle world journey that offers an alternative viewpoint or perspective. Additionally, you may find a teacher or guide in someone who has transitioned out of this life and is currently earthbound.

NOTE: Regarding journeying to the Middle World. We do not recommend such a journey for beginners. There is a risk of meeting earthbound spirits and other entities who may not be helpful. This is not a scare tactic, but a caution for beginners.

All journey work is embarked upon with intention. All the information, everything you may want to know is available and at your fingertips during a journey. As such it is so vast a font of information that focus and intention is key to receiving pertinent information in that moment. Having a clear intention is critical in obtaining information, assistance, or for performing healing work in the Spirit realm in any of the three worlds. Remember that thought is energy, energy is matter, and as you think so you create.

RECIPE 7:

MEASURE THE STRENGTH OF YOUR INTENTION

MATERIALS:

1. Get 2 baby plants: the same kind, same size, and buy them at the same time. (You will see faster results with baby plants.)
2. Relaxing music.

PROCESS:

1. Play soft, relaxing music.
2. Close your eyes.
3. Breathe slowly and deeply three (3) times to relax and tune in with your inner self.
4. Bring your hands into prayer position against your chest at heart level leaving a slight gap between your hands that will be filled with energy.
5. Feel the energy filling the gap between your hands.
6. Carefully pour this energy on one of the plants.
7. Return your hands to prayer position.
8. Breathe again slowly and deeply three (3) times to relax and again tune in with your inner self.
9. Feel the intention of sharing love and feel it fill the gap between your hands.
10. Breath again and fill the space between your hands with love.

11. Carefully pour this love on the other plant.
12. Repeat this exercise for several days or a week and see how the plants grow.

NOTE: Place the plants in a place that will receive the same amount of sunlight and water them the same amount.

Notice if there is a difference between the plants: the one poured over with energy versus the plant poured over with love.

If, after a few days, you notice that the plants are not doing well, dying, or appear to be burned, or are dead it indicates that you are making too much of a mental effort. To fix this feel your effort from your heart instead of your mind. You need to let go and relax. This should be a fun, interesting, and illuminating experiment.

P.S. Get new plants and start over.

RITUAL 4
Elegant – Journey to the Lower World
Detailed Explanation

Although performing and experiencing "journey work" takes practice, with patience and trust in what you receive from Spirit you will find that it is a fairly simple exercise. Be very clear in what your intention is for your journey. Writing down your intention and fine-tuning the words will benefit you and bring you greater clarity during your journey.

You will learn to trust your imagination as a tool to access the Spirit World or non-ordinary reality. Your imagination is not the Spirit World itself. **Remember** that anything is possible in non-ordinary reality, fish can fly, animals can talk, and oceans can be pink.

1. Pick a place large enough to lie down in and where you will feel safe and comfortable and will not be disturbed for about 20 minutes.

NOTE: If you fall asleep easily or you are very tired you can do the journey sitting up.

2. Turn off your phone completely.
3. Wear comfortable clothing, and use a blanket and/or a pillow if that will help you to be as comfortable as possible.

NOTE: This is an exercise that will relax you but you need to guard yourself to not fall asleep. If you fall asleep you will not consciously **Remember** your experience or the information you are given.

4. Feel free to "cleanse" the energy of the room with Sacred Smoke or simply with your intention.

5. Bring in the directions for support and security.

6. Lie down and darken the room, or cover your eyes. Journey work is much easier to do in the dark.

7. Start your drumming CD or have a friend drum or rattle for you.

If you have someone drumming or rattling for you make sure they provide a "call back" by significantly changing the rhythm of the drumming or rattling when your designated time frame is up. A drumming CD created for Journey work will include a "call back".

NOTE: If you have a question regarding your ability to picture, visualize, imagine, or pretend, think about what your mental process is when you are heading towards your car in a large crowded parking lot and you cannot see your car. You still find it, do you not? At least most of the time.

Use your imagination to visualize, picture, or pretend a place, somewhere you have visited, or seen in a film or photograph. This place can be anywhere; a hill, mountain, grasslands, forest, or by the ocean. At this place see an entrance or opening into the ground or water: a hollow tree, an animal burrow, a cave entrance, a man-made opening such as a trapdoor. This will be your entrance to the Lower World. The right entrance for you will feel comfortable and safe. Notice what it looks like and any feelings you may pick up from its look or location.

8. Enter into the opening and notice that you will be in a tunnel.

It may appear dark as you first enter but will lighten as you move through it. The tunnel will angle down slightly or steeply. You will have no trouble walking down the tunnel nor will you feel any fear. Moving through the tunnel may cause you to feel a sense of anticipation. The tunnel may bend or spiral as you travel through it, but it will always lead downwards.

NOTE: Your entrance into the tunnel can be at a walk, you may jump in, you may dive in, or you may fly in. It is up to you. You can count backward from ten to one and then declare yourself in the Lower World or just feel yourself emerge from the tunnel.

9. Within a very short time you will come out of the tunnel and into a landscape.

If you should come out of the tunnel and find yourself in a cave notice what you are seeing and feeling in the cave. It may be that there is something very important to discover in the cave before you leave. Take the time to explore and notice. Then exit the cave into the landscape. You will find an opening or door through which you may exit the cave.

10. Once you have left the tunnel and stepped into the landscape, look around.

It may be a sunny day or a starry night with moonlight. Open all six of your senses to your new environment. Listen, what do you hear; the sound of birds, the wind, water, or? What do you see; forest, desert, mountains, ocean, or? What do you feel; the ground beneath your feet, the bark of a tree, the sifting sand between your toes or? What do you smell; flowers, water, the trees, the ocean, or? What do you taste; salt in the air, the water sweeter than wine, or? What do you sense; movement around you, your Power Animal or Spirit Guide making itself known? Do you have a full awareness of being there, in the Lower World?

It is at this point that you can simply explore the landscape you are in or you may invite your Power Animal or Spirit Guide to make itself known to you. It is said that the first time a Power Animal makes itself known you will see it four times. This may or may not be true for you. If an animal comes forward at your invitation you can dialog with it and find out its purpose or message for you.

NOTE: *Remember* that your Power Animal or Spirit Guide chooses you, not the other way around. For some a visual of the Power Animal or Spirit Guide is possible for others a sense of awareness of the presence of the Power Animal or Spirit Guide takes place. There are different ways of "knowing" something is occurring. Regardless of your perspective you can communicate with your Power Animal or Spirit Guide. Again it can be a very real experience or a form of telepathic communication, where you hear the dialog in your head but not out loud. All methods are valid, there is no wrong way.

11. When you meet your Power Animal or Spirit Guide develop a relationship with him or her or it just as you would any new friend.

Ask what name you should call it. Play with it, feel its fur or feathers, engage it with your attention and love. This is your new BFF (Best Friend Forever). This new friend will be a source of strength, wisdom, and support. Once you have met your Power Animal or Spirit Guide you will be able to access its company and support at any time. It will always be walking with you in all worlds.

You may ask questions of your Power Animal or Spirit Guide, state your original intention for feedback and information, or simply ask for support. Your rapport will grow over time. Each time you journey call your Power Animal or Spirit Guide to join you. You may find that you will have additional Power Animals or Spirit Guides come forward to support different functions of your life. You may find that you develop a whole herd of Power Animals or group of Spirit Guides that become your extended family in the Lower World. Enjoy and trust their company, they are truly wonderful beings and your guardians and protectors. They join with you in a helping and loving way.

12. When you are through visiting the Lower World thank your Power Animal or Spirit Guide and invite them to be with you at all times.

13. Retrace your steps to the tunnel and return to ordinary reality at the time of the "call back."

A Shamanic Way

NOTE: Journal your experience in as much detail as you can ***Remember***. You may find in the writing that the details and the insights gained will become more clear. Writing comes directly out of your subconscious mind and you may find that details will emerge in the writing that you did not initially ***Remember***.

Your time in non-ordinary reality will be like a dream. ***Remembering*** in everyday reality will be very difficult. The details will fade as they do upon waking from a dream. Writing your journey down immediately is very important to be able to retain the information and insights received. The ***Remembering*** will become easier with practice.

A key element in Shamanic practice is the ability to recall the information given in non-ordinary reality and bring it forward into everyday reality. A Shamanic Way is very much in the ***Remember***ing.

Journal Page

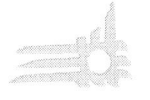

RITUAL 5
Simple – Journey to the Lower World

1. Write down your intention very clearly and concisely.
2. Wear comfortable clothing.
3. Dedicate a space large enough to lie down in.
4. Secure the space from interruption, e.g. turn off the phone.
5. Clear the energy of the space with Sacred Smoke or intention.
6. Start drumming CD.
7. Lie down with eyes covered or in a darkened space.
8. State the intention of your journey four times; silently or out loud.
9. Find your place on Earth for entry to the Lower World.
10. Go to your place of entry to the Lower World.
11. Walk, jump, dive, or fly into the tunnel leading to the Lower World.
12. Count backward from ten to one, if need be, and declare yourself in the Lower World.
13. Notice your surroundings with your six senses: Seeing, Feeling, Tasting, Hearing, Smelling, and Sensing.
14. If this is your first journey, invite your Power Animal or Spirit Guide to come to you.
15. Ask if it is your Power Animal or Spirit Guide and pay attention to the answer as it may not be in words but a feeling.

16. Build a relationship with your Power Animal or Spirit Guide as you would any new friend.

17. State your intention to your Power Animal or Spirit Guide, ask questions, or request support.

18. When the "call back" or drum beat occurs, replay in your mind what has taken place to anchor the memory, and retrace your steps to return to ordinary reality.

19. Journal your experience: your feelings, what your senses noticed, your dialog with your Power Animal or Spirit Guide, and the answers to your questions or intention.

NOTE: The journey is like a dream, incredibly real during its occurrence, but fading over time in ordinary reality. By recording your journeys in a journal or recounted into a voice recorder you will maintain access to the richness of your experience.

If you are 'journeying' with a group of people and desire to share your individual experiences be sure to journal/record your experience before you start the sharing. This will ensure a more complete remembrance.

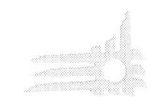

RITUAL 6

Simple – Journey to the Upper World

1. Follow the directions for preparing to access the Lower World.

The difference is your intention is to go to the Upper World and the entrance. It may be a hollow tree that you visualize climbing up inside of, a cave that goes up when you enter it, or perhaps even a pyramid or a mountain which you enter and climb up the inside to the peak.

Another typical way of access is to start in the Lower World and an animal, tree, or mountain will provide access. Perhaps by flying on the back of a bird, or climbing to the top of the tree or mountain.

2. When you reach the top of your access point visualize, picture, imagine, or pretend that you are effortlessly moving upwards to the Upper World.

Remember this world will be a landscape that may be light or dark, or very real feeling or very fantastic feeling. The residents of this Upper World may be the same as you will find in the Lower World. However, typically this is the place of angels and Spirit Guides and teachers of more celestial knowledge. This is also the place of the Akashic records.

NOTE: The **Akashic Records** (akasha is a Sanskrit word meaning "sky", "space" or "aether") is a term used in theosophy and anthroposophy to describe a compendium or library of mystical knowledge encoded in a non-physical plane of existence. These records are described as containing all the knowledge of human experience and the history of the cosmos.

Journal Page

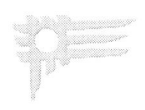

RITUAL 7

Journey To The Middle World
Simple Instruction

1. Follow the directions for preparing to access the Lower World.

The difference is your intention to go to the Middle World and the entrance. The entrances are the same as those to the Lower World and the Upper World however the tunnel will go straight or just up or down a little bit. The access does not gain or lose any significant elevation prior to entering the Middle World landscape.

NOTE: The Middle World is often confusing to the novice journeyer because this is the place that earthbound souls reside. In order to avoid this confusion it is better to journey to the Lower World or Upper World. To ensure that you are not in the Middle World your journey to the Lower or Upper Worlds needs to involve use of a fairly long tunnel either going up or down. This will also ensure a deepened state of awareness in your subconscious mind.

The Middle World is the landscape in which to do what is known as "psycho pump" work. This involves helping earthbound entities to move forward in their journey to the light. It is also the place of performing exorcisms or curse removal, cleansings of negative energies or limpias. This is extremely advanced work and should not be attempted by a beginner.

NOTE: It is important to *Remember* that the primary purpose of a journey is to gain knowledge that is useful in this moment in this reality. Avoid getting lost in the details of non-ordinary reality landscape and inhabitants. Learn to trust the information you receive. Arguing is not a bad thing but at some point giving in to the wisdom of your teacher and then being alert for how things turn out in everyday reality is a key component of Shamanic work. Once again staying conscious of the moment is very important.

Journal Page

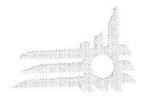

Journal Page

Journal Page

Chapter 6
CHAKRAS

- **Introduction to the Lower 3 Chakras**
- **Introduction to the Heart Chakra (The Bridge)**
- **Introduction to the Upper 3 Chakras**
- **Chakra Attributes & Power Animals** – Key Words
- **Chakra Attributes & Power Animals** – Summary
- **Chakra Attributes & Power Animals** – Chart
- Journal Pages

Chakras wheels of energy
Chakras sublime links to the soul
Chakras bridges to other worlds
Chakras lightbodies eternal and immortal
Chakras sacred gates to Cosmic Will

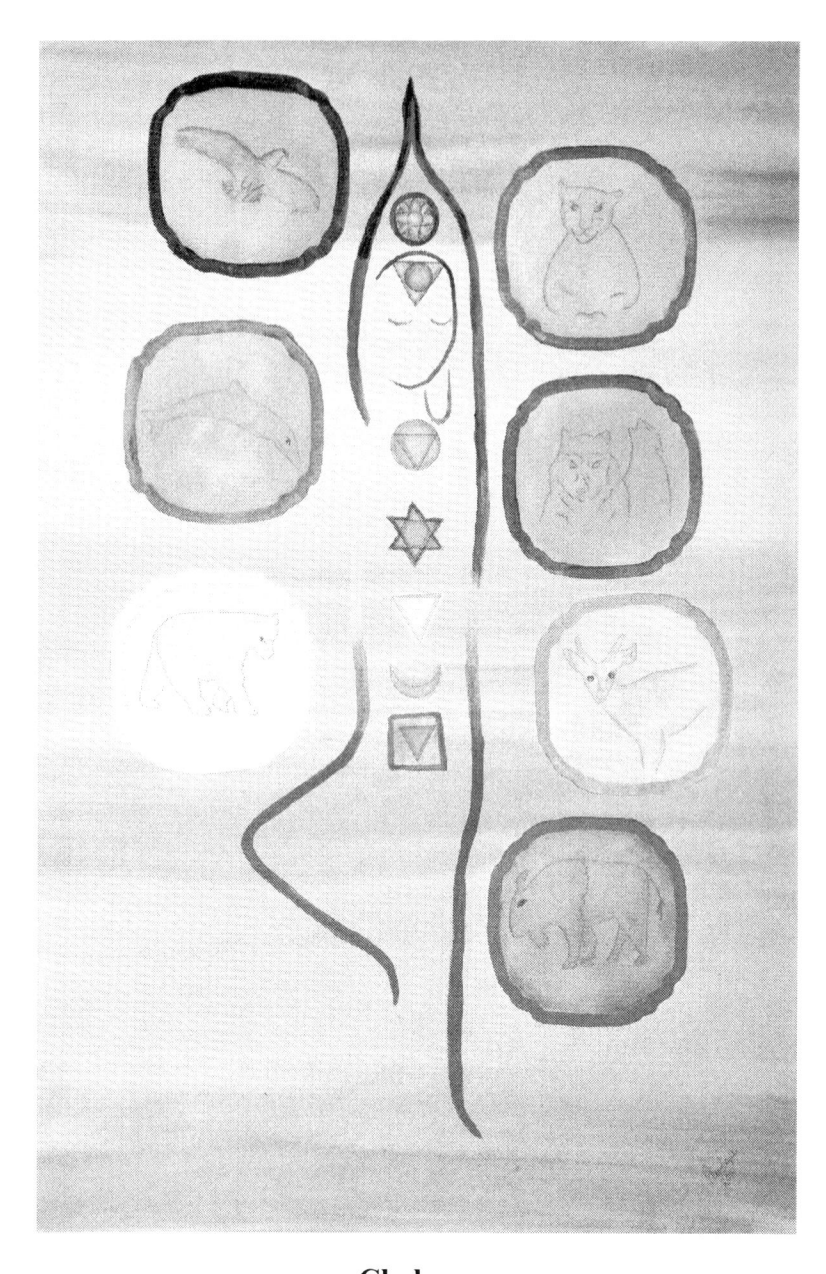

Chakras

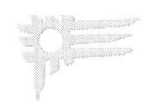

Chapter 6
CHAKRAS

There is much written about Chakras, a Sanskrit term meaning wheel. Simply put they are portals for the energy of the Universe to enter our body, activating it, healing it, energizing it. These portals spin with the energy of the Universe. When these portals are blocked, sluggish, or out of balance usually as the result of a physical, mental, emotional, or Spiritual issue, we experience flagging energy, obstacles in our life path, and health issues: mental, physical, emotional, and or Spiritual.

Although the Chakras are typically regarded as being in the front of the body, they are located along the spine and radiate through the body. Imagine your body as a hollow tube with the chakras lined up within the center of the tube radiating out in all directions. Once again, open, aligned, and freely spinning chakras are essential to our health on multiple levels.

In Shamanic work from the Native American tradition, these seven Chakras have an associated power animal. As you develop your expertise you will find the power animals associated with each chakra that work for you. A guide to get you started is included in <u>*A SHAMANIC WAY*: Rituals, Rattles, and Recipes for Awakening Your Inner Spirit.</u>

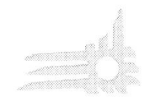

There are many more Chakras than just the seven listed here. In Shamanic practice these other energy portals are opened, balanced, and harmonized as needed. However, this is very advanced healing work and as a primer, *A Shamanic Way* is not designed to delve into such intricacies. Knowledge and understanding of the primary seven Chakras is appropriate for this introductory work. We invite you to journey and experiment in balancing and aligning chakras.

There are seven (7) commonly known Chakras that run along the spine. They are numbered:

7 – Crown – top of head

6 – Brow or third eye – between the eyes

5 – Throat

4 – Heart

3 – Solar plexus – two finger widths above the belly button

2 – Belly or sacral – two finger widths below the belly button

1 – Base or root – at the coccyx level of the spine

Each of these energy portals has a color, a sacred geometry, a specific function – on both an emotional and physical level – and is associated with an element, a sensory channel, and an endocrine gland. They work in harmony with our five bodies – physical, mental, emotional, energetic, and Spiritual.

The seven chakras are divided by the heart chakra. The sacred geometry of the heart chakra illustrates its role as the connector between the lower three and the upper three chakras.

You will notice that the chakras are associated, as they lay along the spine, with various endocrine glands. The endocrine gland system consists of ductless glands which are considered organs. They create various hormones to assist the nervous system in regulating the body's function.

The thymus is often considered an endocrine gland and is associated with the heart chakra, but there is no evidence that it produces a chemical, hormone. The heart itself is a hormone producing endocrine gland.

INTRODUCTION
LOWER THREE CHAKRAS:
1ST, ROOT; 2ND, SACRAL; 3RD, SOLAR PLEXUS

The lower three chakras are associated with material and physical issues. They tend to be ruled by the EGO. What is the EGO you may ask? Essentially the EGO is the part of our mind that identifies us as being the sum of things outside of ourselves. It is known to some as an acronym for "Edging God Out".

These include our possessions, the work we do, our social status and recognition, our knowledge and education, physical appearance, personal and family history, belief systems which include: religious, political, nationalistic, racial, and other collective identifications, special abilities, and relationships. Defining our sense of worth with use of this type of measurement device is the job of our EGO.

It is unfortunate that often we do not go beyond this type of evaluation. For some, this is EVERYTHING. Such a lack of understanding ourselves as spiritual beings experiencing a physical existence tends to produce negative results. In such cases, fear is often prevalent and a sense of lack or incompleteness is present despite our accomplishments and material wealth.

This EGO is in charge of our mind in this situation. The endless mental chatter, or squirrel brain (the squirrel running endlessly on its wheel), is in charge. The EGO causes us to worry about the future, even though it is not yet here, and to anguish and fret over the past, which is long gone. The EGO causes us to miss out on the PRESENT because we are not in the moment at any time except perhaps briefly at the best of times. The fear, the worry, the regret tends to pull us away from our PRESENT.

Our EGO serves a vital purpose, keeping us alive at the basic level. It is when the EGO takes full control that we feel a gaping hole in our inner self. Some of us try to fill it by overachievement, anger and blaming, shopping, eating, depression and giving up, and the list goes on and on.

The lower three chakras are essential to the alignment of our physical, mental, emotional, energetic, and spiritual bodies. However for them to be balanced and spinning freely is critical in maintaining our EGO in its rightful place. If they are blocked, sluggish, murky, or unbalanced these three lower chakras will interfere with the alignment and balance of the rest of the chakra system.

1ST – ROOT Chakra,
Base of the Spine

ATTRIBUTES: Red, Inverted Pyramid within a Square, North, Survival, Earth, Ovaries/Testes, Buffalo, Oak, Ruby.

The first chakra is located at the base of our spine and connects us to earth.

It is truly a root anchoring us to Mother Earth. A well balanced Root chakra provides us with feelings of well being and a sense of security. This chakra is aligned with the material world and survival.

When the Root chakra is unbalanced and not well aligned, feelings of anger, depression, and issues in the material world like money will be felt.

This is the "Foundation" chakra for the other six chakras and needs to be strong, firmly balanced, and well grounded to support the alignment of the other chakras.

NOTE: Depression is anger not expressed outwardly but turned inwardly to self.

2ND – SACRAL Chakra,

Sacrum

ATTRIBUTES: Orange, Horizontal Crescent, South, Sexual, Fire, Pancreas, Deer, Bright Flowers, Amber.

The second chakra is located at the sacrum, that large triangular bone in your lower back between your hip bones and the base of the spine. You can easily locate it by placing two finger widths below your navel.

The Sacral chakra is associated with creativity, sexuality, fertility, and pleasure in the material world. The Sacral chakra is our connection to our physical body. When this chakra is aligned and balanced we feel joy, creativity, and the carnal pleasures of food, sex, and passion are fully enjoyed. This is a chakra connected to joy of living and all acts of living our physical life.

If this chakra is not fully open and spinning we experience fear, depression and a lack of ambition and creativity.

The balance of this "Joy of Living" chakra is essential for us to experience life with childlike innocence and passion.

NOTE: Depression is anger not expressed outwardly but turned inwardly to self.

3RD – SOLAR PLEXUS Chakra,
Top of Stomach below Ribs

ATTRIBUTES: Yellow, Inverted Pyramid, East, Personal Power, Air, Adrenals, Bear, Blooming Tropicals, Topaz.

The third chakra is located under your rib cage at the top of your stomach, approximately 2 finger widths above navel.

The Solar Plexus chakra is associated with personal power, self-esteem, and creating and manifesting our dreams. When the third chakra is open, balanced, and spinning freely we feel a sense of personal power. The ability to set and accomplish goals is actualized. We feel vital and alive within ourselves and our place in the world. We are able to accept our own responsibility for our actions, the results, and our reactions.

If the Solar Plexus chakra is blocked we will feel stuck, without focus or energy to do anything creative. We may feel dis-empowered and find we are blaming others and situations for our 'lot in life'.

This "Power" chakra's optimum alignment and balance is essential to our sense of personal power and self-regard.

NOTE: Going with your 'gut feeling' is being in touch with your 3rd chakra.

As a Shamanic practitioner you need to be aware that the entities of the Middle World are particularly attracted to the 1st, 2nd, and 3rd chakras and as such can grab hold of those chakras and create problems for you. This is yet another reason not to enter the Middle World. Shamanic practice is very much about the healing of the soul and the energetic body, therefore aligning and balancing chakras is an integral part of that healing work.

INTRODUCTION
HEART CHAKRA – The Bridge

CHAKRA COLORS

The Heart chakra serves as a bridge or connection between the lower and upper chakras. You will notice the heart feels, on a physical level, the energy of the lower three chakras. On the emotional level the heart feels the energy of the upper three chakras. This merger is symbolized by the Sacred Geometry of the interlocking pyramid, one inverted and one right side up. Together they make a six-pointed star. Each point indicates one of the six chakras embodied within the Heart chakra.

There is a phrase, "The Listening Heart". In listening with your heart you are listening with your energetic being.

You will notice that the Heart chakra color is associated with the color green. Green is a bridge between the warm colors of the lower chakras: red, orange, and yellow, and the cooler colors of the upper chakras: turquoise/blue, indigo, and purple. Take note of how the colors merge with each other as they move up through the chakra system beginning with the red of the Root chakra.

Red of the Root chakra and the yellow of the Solar Plexus make orange of the Sacral chakra. The Sacral chakra is an expression of balance between the Root chakra and its role in our survival and the Solar Plexus chakra with its energy of personal power.

The indigo blue of the Third Eye and green of the Heart merge to make the turquoise/blue of the Throat chakra. Speaking our truth is a merging of the balance of the Heart and the Third Eye.

The indigo of the Third Eye and purple of the Crown chakras stand apart. These upper two chakras are intricately linked yet separate. The Third Eye connects the invisible world within us and around us. The Crown chakra connects us directly with Spirit and the energy of the Universe.

NOTE: In some traditions the colors associated with the Crown chakra may also be violet (light purple), white, or gold. Again, as you practice you will find the chakra colors that resonate with you personally.

4TH – HEART Chakra,
Heart

ATTRIBUTES: Green, Interlocked Pyramid creating a Six Pointed Star, West, Emotions, Water, Heart, Wolf, Evergreens, Malachite.

The fourth chakra is located at your heart.

The Heart chakra is associated with emotions. It acts as a connection between the lower three chakras which deal with the material/physical world and the upper three which deal with the cerebral world of communication, wisdom, and spirituality. The 4th chakra expresses the attributes of the other chakras. It can sing with joy felt on a spiritual or love level. It can feel broken and painful as a result of un-attained dreams or betrayed trust.

When we cry, if the tears flow unimpeded, they will fall from our face to our chest (heart) in an effort to heal. When our heart is full of love and joy it may feel as though it could 'just burst'.

The term 'follow your heart' refers to paying attention to how your Heart chakra feels about something.

NOTE: Maintaining an open "Bridge" chakra will generate your personal magnetism out to the world in a healing way. It will also allow your magnetism to attract the right people, the right situations, and the right material wealth to you. Having this reciprocal effect is an unintended consequence of having a balanced well aligned Heart chakra.

INTRODUCTION
UPPER THREE CHAKRAS:
5TH THROAT; 6TH THIRD EYE; 7TH CROWN

The upper three chakras are associated with communication, inner wisdom, and Spiritual connection. As stated earlier chakras are spinning portals for energy to enter and exit from our physical body. The upper chakras define our essence as spiritual beings. We speak from the heart, we follow our intuition, and we feel our connection to Spirit and to everything and everyone on earth.

When 9/11/2001 occurred the entire world felt the effects of that tragic event. People all over the globe were crying for those who perished and those left behind. This was a connection that knew no bounds because we felt the energy of the event and the effects of that event. This is a vivid example of how the upper three chakras respond to energetic stimulation.

Fortunately we do not have to experience anything as profoundly tragic as the events of 9/11 to engage our upper three chakras. If we pay attention we will notice these chakras vibrating with awareness on a regular basis as we go about our daily lives. Again this is very much about staying in the moment.

5TH – THROAT Chakra,

Base of Throat

ATTRIBUTES: Turquoise/blue, Inverted Pyramid within a Circle, Below, Speech, Thyroid, Dolphin, Wildflowers, Aquamarine.

The fifth chakra is located at your throat, at your voice box.

The Throat chakra is associated with communication. When we speak we are attempting to communicate. We use words, song, or sounds. Having an open 5th chakra means it is connected to the heart. Communication comes from the heart or through 'heartfelt words'. If the Throat chakra is blocked words tend to be just words. We have 'no voice'. We want to 'reach out and touch someone' on a regular basis and speaking is our primary vehicle. However, how many of us think (check with our heart) before we speak, particularly in a negatively charged emotional situation such as anger, fear, sorrow, frustration?

Maintaining an open Throat chakra relies upon alignment with an open Heart chakra. Only then will we truly find our 'voice' and be able to speak our 'truth'. Words are incredibly powerful. Words can never be 'taken back'. They move our thoughts out into the physical world. Words have energy that affects the world.

If you have any doubt of the effects of words, spoken, written, or thought, on the physical world, check out the art of Dr. Masaru Emoto's *Hidden Messages in Water*. He photographed ice crystals that were subjected to words on a piece of paper such as love, war, thank you, hate. The crystals reacted to the words and the images he captured demonstrate the inexplicable relationship of words on our physical world.

NOTE: The balance of your "Voice" chakra is critical for articulating your heart and your wisdom, in turn affecting the world in a positive way.

6TH – THIRD EYE Chakra,
Middle of Forehead

ATTRIBUTES: Indigo (Color of the midnight sky), Inverted Pyramid Enclosing a Circle, Within, Wisdom, Pituitary, Cougar, Rose, Sodalite.

The sixth chakra is located at your forehead, 1" above your brow line between your eyes.

The sixth chakra is the seat of our intuitive wisdom. We use our five senses on a daily basis; to see, feel, hear, taste, and smell the world around us. The sixth sense of intuition opens our awareness to the unseen world and the wisdom of our innate sense.

If everything is energy and energy is everywhere, then using intuitive abilities will allow us to glean wisdom from that which is not apparent to our five senses. We all have this ability. We are born with this gift of inner awareness. Children are very comfortable with their intuitive sense. Unfortunately over time as children mature, it becomes covered up and buried beneath the indoctrination of societal acceptances, taboos, and overall compliance with society.

Our Third Eye is very open during our dream time, Shamanic experience, and meditation. Some call this Wisdom, the 6th Sense, Intuition, or Psychic Ability. Regardless of what it is called we all have the ability and the means to develop consciously. Using meditation, recording our dreams, listening to our heart and body and how it reacts to people and situations, learning to trust what we feel; all are ways to develop and strengthen our Sixth Sense.

NOTE: Keeping your "Wisdom" chakra open, balanced, and aligned with your other chakras will reveal a new world to you on many levels.

7ᵀᴴ – CROWN Chakra,
Top of Head

ATTRIBUTES: Purple/Violet/White, Lotus Blossom, Above, Connection to Spirit, Pineal, Eagle, Blossoming Trees, Purple Sapphire.

The seventh chakra is located at the top of your head. This is the place on your skull called the fontanelle, better known as the soft spot. This is the last place on the skull to close after being born.

The seventh chakra connects us to the Universe, to Spirit, to God, to the Infinite, to the Divine. Whatever word you are comfortable with which denotes the Universal Good, this is that place of connection. The Crown chakra is our opening to our spiritual self. This connection to the Divine is simply DIVINE. It is our ability to be in the moment without regret of the past or fear of the future. To simply BE.

NOTE: Having an open "Being" chakra allows us to experience the light essence of God. It is all knowing and everlasting. When our Crown chakra is open wide, spinning freely and the other six chakras are aligned and open our life is enriched, enhanced, and healthy.

CHAKRAS
ATTRIBUTES: Key Words
POWER ANIMAL
COLOR, ELEMENT, FUNCTION, SENSORY CHANNEL

NOTE: The attributes of the chakras are as personal as the attributes of the directions. With practice you will find those that resonate with you. Be open and alert for the energy to make itself known. The list below is typical but may not be typical for you. This is simply a guide to help you get started.

(1) Base-BUFFALO

Red

Earth

Ground to Mother Earth

Smell

<u>Respect the Alchemy of Earth</u>. Honors Earth.

(2) Sacral-DEER

Orange

Water

Survival

Taste

<u>Personal Needs and Survival</u>. Care of self as separate physical entity; acknowledges and allows sacred life force to manifest within; promotes healing energy for self and others.

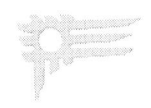

(3) Solar Plexus-BEAR
Yellow
Fire
Personal Power
Sight

Self-Awareness. Personal growth and stands in one's own power; transition and change through introspection; recognizing the limits of human knowing; having the power of humility and forgiveness.

(4) Heart-WOLF
Green
Air
Love
Touch

The Ability to Love and Care for Others and for Oneself. Awareness of community and of relationships; joy in nurturing and supporting others and receiving same from others.

(5) Throat-DOLPHIN
(or Personal Power Animal)
Turquoise/Blue
Ether
Communication
Sound

The Discovery of One's Own Voice. Defines how best to use personal gifts, learning to distinguish between personal power, power over others, or another's power over you; honors the gift of power with courage.

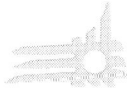

(6) Brow-MOUNTAIN LION/COUGAR
Indigo (Midnight Sky)
Mind
Intuition
Thought

Wisdom. Differentiates between human knowledge and universal truth, with openness to lessons of the elders and recognizes the forces and truths that govern our lives and all others.

(7) Crown-EAGLE
Purple/Violet/White
Spirit
Oneness with the Universe
Experience

The Ability to see the Big Picture. Balance between earth beings and Spirit, with an awareness that the Earth journey is not separate from our spiritual identity.

Chakras
Summary

The **lower three chakras** are involved in physical attributes of our lives; survival, reproduction/procreation, and personal power.

The **heart connects** above and below.

The **upper three chakras** are involved in communication, thought, and connection to Spirit.

The **1st** and **2nd** chakras are principally concerned with receiving into the body two forces which come into it at the physical level – spent fire from the earth at the **1st** and vitality from the sun at the **2nd**.

3rd, **4th**, and **5th** chakras are engaged with forces which reach us through our personality; the lower astral in the **3rd** chakra, the higher astral in the **4th**, and the lower mind in the **5th** chakras.

The **6th** and **7th** chakras stand apart and are directly linked to inner wisdom or higher mind and Spirit, respectively.

NOTE: This chakra information is provided because it is useful in a Shamanic practice. Balancing and aligning the chakras is a key component to moving forward with healing work.

Remember that chakra alignment and balance is significant in promoting health and well being however this is only a part of what is needed for living life in a healthy and abundant way:

To Be All You Were Created To Be.

Journal Page

Journal Page

Journal Page

Journal Page

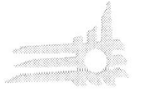

CHAKRAS AND KEY ATTRIBUTES

Chakra	Color	Sacred Geometry	Direction	Sensory	Element	Endocrine Gland	Animal Totem	Plant Totem	Mineral Totem	Disorder	Emotional Disturbance
1st Root Base of Spine	Red	Inverted Pyramid within a Square	North	Survival	Earth	Ovaries/Testes	Buffalo Link to Earth	Oak	Ruby	Anger; Rage; Frustration; Depression; Fatigue	Fear of death; Impotence/Frigidity; Abandonment Issues
2nd Sacral Sacrum	Orange	Horizontal Crescent	South	Sexual	Fire	Pancreas	Deer Strength Through Gentleness	Bright flowers	Amber	Fear; Repression; Digestive Issues; Diabetes	Violation of Personal Space; Molestation; Impotence/Frigidity;
3rd Solar Plexus 2" below the Navel	Yellow	Inverted Pyramid	East	Personal Power	Air	Adrenals	Bear Power	Blooming Tropicals	Topaz	Mental Overload; Poor Circulation; Intestinal Issues	Fear: of Losing Control; of Relationships; Inability to Accept/Receive
4th Heart	Green	Interlocked Pyramids = Six Pointed Star	West	Emotions	Water	Heart	Wolf Peace with Self	Evergreens	Malachite	Jealousy; Greed; Resistance; Envy; Ulcers; Heart Palpations	Genetic/Ancient Memory Grief, Helplessness; Shame; Disillusionment;
5th Base of Throat	Turquoise	Inverted Pyramid within a Circle	Below	Speak		Thyroid	Dolphin Communication with Others	Wildflowers	Aquamarine	Passivity; Isolation: Possessiveness; Throat and Respiratory Issues	Inability to Speak Personal Truth/Feelings; Lack of Trust; Lack of Nurturing

126

CHAKRAS

CHAKRAS AND KEY ATTRIBUTES

Chakra	Color	Sacred Geometry	Direction	Sensory	Element	Endocrine Gland	Animal Totem	Plant Totem	Mineral Totem	Disorder	Emotional Disturbance
6th Third Eye 1" above brow line of forehead, between the eyes	Indigo Blue (Color of the Midnight Sky)	Inverted Pyramid Enclosing a Circle	Within	Wisdom		Pituitary	Cougar Courage to See	Rose	Sodalite	Arrogance; Conceit; Totalitarianism; Irritability; Upper Respiratory and Headache Issues; Mental Stress; Nervousness	Denying Personal Truth; Not Following Your Path; Ignoring/Distrusting Your Inner Voice;
7th Crown Skull Fontanelle (Soft Spot)	Purple/Violet/White	Lotus Blossom	Above	Connection to Spirit		Pineal	Eagle See Great Distances	Blossoming Trees	Purple Sapphire	Overexcitement; Nerves; Depression; Creative Exhaustion; Lowered immune system; Insomnia; Migraines; Bladder/Kidney Issues	Denying Your Purpose; Rebelling Against Your Truth

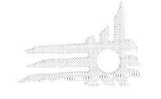

127

Journal Page

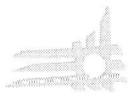

Journal Page

Journal Page

Chapter 7

RITUALS & CEREMONIES

- **Recipe 8** – Key Points In Creating Ritual
- **Ritual 8** – Prosperity
- **Recipe 9** – Prayer Stick
- **Energy Clearing / Removing Blocks**
- **Ritual 9** – Energy Clearing for a Person
- **Ritual 10** – Energy Clearing for a Building or Business
- **Ritual 11** – House Blessing
- Journal Pages

Ritual & Ceremony, Celebrate Life
Ritual & Ceremony, Honor the Universe
Ritual & Ceremony, Energize the Soul
Ritual & Ceremony, Focus the Spirit
Ritual & Ceremony,
Transcend Our Physical and Mental Space
Ritual & Ceremony, Support our Change

Celebrate

Chapter 7
RITUALS & CEREMONIES

Rituals & ceremonies are a means to welcome Spirit or God into your life. A ritual can be as simple as the ceremony of saying grace before your meal, or as complex as a rite of passage ceremony for a child, a marriage, or for a loved one who has passed on. A ritual simply says, *"Welcome. Bless me and this time. I honor you in all your glory and treasure your presence in my life. Come to me now for there is always room in my heart for you."*

Rituals are celebrations of Spirit and our ability to connect from the heart to something greater than we are. Ritual is something that we have in common as human beings regardless of our background, our culture, or our heritage. Rituals can be performed privately or in a group. Birthday celebrations, weddings, and memorial services are rituals typically performed by a community linked heart to heart. Prayer and meditation are rituals usually performed privately. Ritual can be applied to almost any occasion depending on the intention of the participants. A house blessing, a naming ceremony, an energy clearing of a building or a person, the list is limited only by imagination.

Shamanic ritual utilizes that awareness of the energies and the interconnectedness of the earth, Spirit world, and the participants. This type of ritual uses a process called a "journey" (a type of altered state) performed by the Shamanic practitioner to "travel" to the Spirit world; a "world" or "dimension" usually only accessed through dreams, mythology, and near death experiences. Over time the term Shamanism has come to refer to the practitioner's process.

Depending on the type of ritual, the Shamanic practitioner may use the sound of a drum, rattle, or other means to enter an altered type state to access "non-ordinary reality" or Spirit world. This is the place of accessing healing processes, problem solving, and where other opportunities lie to maximize the abilities of the human mind. A typical opening portion of a Shamanic ritual calls in the power of the cardinal directions: North, East, South, and West, each of which have specific energetic attributes, using drumming, rattling, songs, or other means.

Utilizing A Shamanic Way in rituals and ceremonies that we traditionally perform such as birthdays, weddings, and other rites of passage creates a tangible link between the energies of Spirit and the participants, adding dimension and depth to the celebration.

RITUALS & CEREMONIES

There are many ways to design rituals and ceremonies in A Shamanic Way. We provide you with examples upon which you may build, tailor, or simply use. You will find with practice that all rituals and ceremonies will become uniquely your own. All rituals and ceremonies are anchored in prayer otherwise known as "intention".

Consider if prayers are sent to Spirit by our thoughts, then our thoughts must be prayers. If this is true and thoughts are prayers, what have you been praying all day?

Thoughts are incredibly powerful and stimulate our connection to Spirit, our creativity, and the Law of Magnetic Attraction.

Journal Page

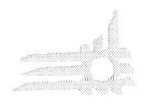

RECIPE 8:

KEY POINTS TO KEEP IN MIND WHEN CREATING A RITUAL OR CEREMONY

1. It is important to learn how to release your intention once it is formed.

Consider that your intention or your prayer as placing your order with the Universe. If you keep asking, the Universe cannot provide until you finish your order.

2. Be humble in your prayer and keep your ego low.

Your ego wants you to stay stuck in the past or worry about the future. Be aware of the relentless negative self talk from the ego. It is in the NOW that magic happens.

3. Maintain an attitude of gratitude.

Gratitude is like a cleanser for your negative energy. As it dissolves the negative energy the Universe will provide.

4. Recognize that you are a magnet of energy drawing to you everything in your life.
5. Be alert to the manifestation of your intention as it may come about in a very unexpected way and time.
6. Know your limitations and work on them to expand, alter, or change them.

Remember if your subconscious cannot accept your intention your energy will not draw it in to you.

Journal Page

RITUAL 8
Ritual of Blessings of/for Prosperity

Prosperity can be many things not just Financial Abundance. You chose. Is it Financial Abundance? Is it Prosperity in positive thought? How about Prosperity in friends and family-those you can count upon? And of course there is Prosperity in Health. You choose.

Create your Sacred Circle following the instructions previously outlined in this book.

1. Create a Sacred Circle sprinkling cornmeal and tobacco to delineate the Circle.

Cornmeal represents the abundance of the earth. Tobacco is a vehicle for transmitting prayers to Spirit.

2. Decorate your Sacred Circle with items that are meaningful to you and reflect your intention for ceremony. Pay attention to positioning items in the place of the four directions.
3. Create an alter space within your Sacred Circle that holds items symbolic to you for prosperity.
4. Include a prayer stick or prayer ties that you have infused with your prayers.

The recipe for creating a prayer stick or prayer ties follows this section. You may also create a prayer stick or prayer ties within your Sacred Circle as part of your ceremony.

5. Smudge yourself with Sacred Smoke.
6. Smudge your Sacred Circle, altar space, and other items within the Circle with Sacred Smoke.

RITUALS & CEREMONIES

7. Call in the directions.

8. Sit or stand within your Sacred Circle and enter a meditative prayer state.

At this time you have prepared yourself and your Sacred Space for your intention.

9. **THIS IS THE MOST IMPORTANT STEP!!**
   Say your prayers FOR PROSPERITY with high emotion and with the <u>KNOWLEDGE THAT IT IS SO</u>.

Remember to maintain an ATTITUDE OF GRATITUDE. Giving thanks in advance is a powerful tool.

Avoid using prayer statements that reflect negative emotion such as fear, despair, anger, or what you DO NOT WANT.

Phrasing in Shamanic Work is **very important** whether it is in your prayers or in forming your intention for your Journey Work.

WORDS & THOUGHTS ARE INCREDIBLY POWERFUL.
WORDS & THOUGHTS ARE ENERGY.
WORDS & THOUGHTS HAVE MATTER/SUBSTANCE.
WORDS & THOUGHTS MANIFEST YOUR REALITY.

10. Upon completion of your prayers with focused intention <u>***Let Them Go***</u> (this means stop thinking about them).

NOTE: *Remember* if you keep placing your order again and again the Universe cannot provide until you are done.

11. Closing the Ritual. Follow the same instructions for closing your Sacred Circle as previously described in Chapter 3, Step 15.

RECIPE 9:

PRAYER STICK

Create a prayer stick or a sequence of twenty-two, forty-four, or sixty-six prayer ties or both a prayer stick and prayer ties. This will anchor and hold your prayers beyond the time of your actual ritual.

Create them beforehand and place them within your Sacred Circle or incorporate their creation into your ceremony. This will bless them and energize them for when your ceremony is over.

NOTE: By creating a prayer stick or prayer ties you will be putting your prayers out of you and into this receptacle allowing you to fully LET GO as is done in ceremonies like the sacred Sun Dance.

Materials:
1. Stick, piece of wood, branch, or a tree.
2. Feathers, ribbons, beads, charms, paint, etc.

Methods:
1. Choose a piece of wood that speaks to you.

(You will find one upon declaring your intention. Simply pay attention to what presents itself. This is another example of being in the moment.)

2. Smudge it with Sacred Smoke and honor it with a blessing.
3. Decorate it in any manner that works for you, feathers, rocks, paint, beads, etc. Allow Spirit to guide you.

(You may choose to drape your Prayer Ties on your Prayer Stick.)

4. Once it is completed and you have placed it in a special location Smudge it again with Sacred Smoke, blessing it and thanking it for holding your prayers.

(Incorporating your Prayer Stick into your altar or Sacred Space is often chosen for placement. Your Prayer Stick can be placed anywhere. It can be as subtle as an ornament for your house or as dedicated as a focal point of your Sacred Space.)

Energy Clearing

Everything is energy and everything is connected. We are electromagnetic beings. If you want to really simplify this thought consider our physical body as a machine that is activated by energy. Our environment and society causes many blocks or intrusions in the energy field that animates our bodies, emotions, and spirit.

This is the place some call our aura, some call the grid, some call it the lightbody. This is the part of the body that is activated by the chakras and our relationship to Universal energy and the molecular makeup of our physical selves.

Consider that all beliefs and thought create the electromagnetic field surrounding you. What are you attracting to yourself with your thought, your electromagnetic attraction?

Living life in A Shamanic Way alerts us to our energy field. We may feel a block or intrusion because physically we do not feel well, or mentally our mind is flitting around with a million thoughts and no focus, or emotionally we feel fragile and vulnerable.

The symptoms of blocked energy are too numerous to discuss. However, once you allow yourself to experience life in A Shamanic Way, you will notice when you need to clear your energy, a building's energy, a business's energy, or a favorite animal's energy. You will learn to trust Spirit, the little voice in your head and heart that guides you through your life.

There are as many ways to clear blocked energy as there is imagination. We offer you a few examples to learn from, work with, and build upon.

The simplest way to clear minor blockages is to Smudge with Sacred Smoke. **Remember** to check if use of smoke is alright with the person or place you are working on. If you choose to perform this simple clearing and it involves a place or another person, be sure to Smudge yourself first and last. (You will want to clear off any energy you may have picked up during your ritual.)

Using a drum or rattle can also clear energy.

A complete ceremony can be performed if you would like to have a more elegant ritual.

Journal Page

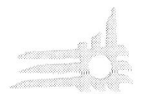

RITUAL 9
Energy Clearing for a Person

1. Smudge yourself and then the person.
2. Create a Sacred Circle or Space.
3. Have them lay down within a Sacred Space or Circle.
4. Position them with their head in the East and their feet in the West.
5. East holds the energy of new beginnings, and the West holds the energy of spiritual illumination.
6. Pray over them and rattle, drum, or brush with a feather to raise their energetic body to the surface.
7. Use your hands about 6" above their body to feel for hotspots or coldspots in their energetic field.
8. When you encounter one of these spots use a feather, rattle, or drumming to balance the energy.

You may not be able to read the energetic field in this way. You can also check the chakras.

<u>You can check the person's chakras with a pendulum.</u> Wrap the chain of a pendulum looselyaround your finger and allow the pendulum to hover above the person's chakras about 3"-6".

NOTE: Anything can be used as a pendulum. It simply needs to have a chain of some type with a weight that will hold it straight down. This means it could be a crystal on a chain, a piece of wood, a necklace, even a key on a chain. It simply needs to be light enough to move with the energy, long enough to garner movement, and heavy enough to be taut when hanging it down loosely. A chunk of keys on a short chain will NOT work. Use logic but know there are no hard and fast rules.

RITUALS & CEREMONIES

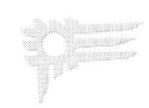

1. Start at the crown chakra. (See illustration in Chapter 4) If the chakra is blocked the pendulum will either remain still, become a little jerky, move in a back and forth motion, a side to side motion, or an elliptical motion. The goal is to have the pendulum moving in a circle.

2. If you encounter a blocked chakra, keep the pendulum position over the chakra and with intention command the chakra to open, you may also blow lightly towards the chakra with your intention for the chakra to open. (Drumming or rattling, toning over the chakra will also assist in unblocking it.)

NOTE: Keep in mind that everything is energy, and energy is a vibration. Toning is essentially a vibration that you physically inject into the chakra or any other place that may hold blocked energy. You simply put your mouth close to the area of blockage and allow Spirit to use your voice to create the vibration. Typically as an "Ah" (***Remember*** Spirit is using you as a tool so your tone may come out as something other than "AH") held until you need to take a breath. You may need to do this several times, then check with the pendulum if the blockage has cleared.

3. With time the pendulum will begin circling. Maintain the position until the circle is about 4"-8" in diameter. Then move to the next chakra.

NOTE: It is not unusual for the chakras to be only 2" or 3" in diameter at first. This is not optimal but better than stuck. With work and repeated clearings the chakras will open to the optimal 4" to 8" diameter.

Once all the chakras are open use a feather, singing, toning, rattling, or drumming to anchor the energetic body in the open position.

NOTE: You choose the anchor method best suited to you and to the person you are working on. There are as many ways as there is imagination. Reiki, Tibetan cymbals, a rain stick, etc. are some other ideas for your consideration.

There are many other ways to clear, balance, and re-energize a person's energetic body in A Shamanic Way. These are just a few.

Journal Page

RITUAL 10
Clearing the Energy of a Building or Business

1. Circle the outside of the building (if possible) in a counter-clockwise manner with drumming, Sacred Smoke, rattling, and or singing. In the case of these options not being viable, you can use a little tobacco, or crumbled sage or cedar with intention and lightly sprinkle it as you walk through the building or office.
2. Circle the building three times.
3. You are moving the stagnant energy out of the magnetic field.
4. Then move through the building circling each room in a counter-clockwise manner with drumming, Sacred Smoke, rattling, and or singing. Circle each room three times or use the more discreet method as described above.
5. Reverse your direction, thus bringing in new energy to each room. Circle each room three times in a clockwise direction.

NOTE: You may want to clear out all the old stagnant energy of the property before you bring in new, fresh energy.

6. When the interior has been cleared and re-energized; circle the outside of the building (if possible) in a clockwise manner with drumming, Sacred Smoke, rattling, and or singing.
7. Circle the building three times bringing new and vibrant energy into the building from the outside.

8. As always your intention holds the prayer and subsequently the energy you are both moving out and the new energy you are bringing in.

Have people who occupy the building join you in the ritual if you so desire and they want to participate. Give them some type of percussion instrument that you have Smudged with Sacred Smoke.

NOTE: Instruments can be as simple as two rocks or two sticks that can be tapped together or even simply clapping your hands with intention. *Remember* to Smudge your participants with Sacred Smoke, but always ask permission first. Some people may be allergic to smoke or may have an adverse reaction.

RITUAL 11
House Blessing

1. Follow the Energy Clearing ritual for a building.
2. At the conclusion of bringing in new energy to each room say a blessing specific to the function of that room.

Have the people who live in the house contribute their prayers and wishes for each room before moving on to the next room.

For instance: in the kitchen, the blessing could be for joy in cooking, healthy food, delicious food, or in the bedroom, the blessing could be for refreshing sleep, a rejuvenating sanctuary, etc.

3. Upon conclusion of bringing in new energy to the house and property, for the closing ritual that takes place outside, have the prayers pertain to the bigger picture: a happy home, prosperity and abundance in all things, etc.

Journal Page

Journal Page

Journal Page

Journal Page

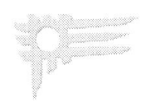

Chapter 8

BREATHING & MEDITATION

- **Recipe 10** – For Living a Full & Blessed Life
- **Brain Activity**
- **Recipe 11** – Complete Breathing
- **Recipe 12** – Circular Breathing
- **Recipe 13** – Rhythmic Breathing
- **Recipe 14** – Cleansing Breath
- **Recipe 15** – Simple Meditation
- **Recipe 16** – Unified Chakra Meditation
- Journal Pages

Breathe in the life force of the Universe
Center the mind in the heart
Hear the heartbeat of Spirit
Open the heart with each breath
Bridge the gap between yourself and Spirit
Breathe
Allow Spirit to wash over you, through you,
And out of you to the World

BREATHING & MEDITATION

You may ask what does breathing and meditation have to do with A Shamanic Way? We say to you, pretty much everything. Besides the obvious, without breath you have death. Both breathing properly and meditating activates the electrical activity of the brain and the energetic body of "the body". Each works independently, but when deliberately combined they create a powerful force.

Living life in A Shamanic Way requires practices in addition to Rituals, Shamanic Journeys, and using Sacred Tools. To "Awaken Your Inner Spirit" takes work on all levels of your life; eating healthy food, abstaining from substances that remove yourself from yourself, maintaining positive thought, being a compassionate person, breathing with benefit, and meditating for your "peace of mind" are just some of the extracurricular, though critical, aspects of living life in A Shamanic Way.

There are as many extracurricular activities to enhance a positive life experience as imagination and creative thought can summon.

Meditation

The brain is an electrochemical organ using electromagnetic energy to function. During meditation brain waves alter. An **electroencephalograph** is the instrument used to record the brain's spontaneous electrical activity.

Brainwaves are categorized by their frequency and amplitude. They range from the high amplitude, low frequency **delta** to the low amplitude, high frequency **beta**. These characteristic brainwaves are consistent across gender, age, cultural and geographic boundaries.

Brain Wave Activity During Meditation

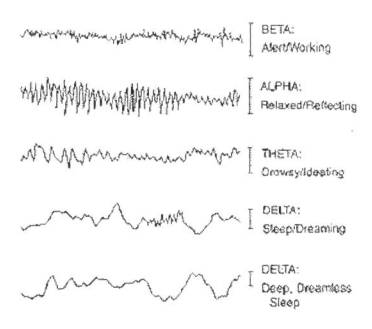

~~	BETA: Alert/Working
~~	ALPHA: Relaxed/Reflecting
~~	THETA: Drowsy/Ideating
~~	DELTA: Sleep/Dreaming
~~	DELTA: Deep, Dreamless Sleep

BETA – 13-30 cycles per second – awaking awareness, extroversion, concentration, logical thinking – active conversation. The normal waking state. A debater would be in high beta. A person making a speech, or a teacher, or a talk show host would all be in beta when they are engaged in their work.

ALPHA – 7-13 cycles per second – relaxation times, non-arousal, meditation, hypnosis

THETA – 4-7 cycles per second – day dreaming, dreaming, creativity, meditation, hypnosis, paranormal phenomena, out of body experiences, extra sensory perception (ESP), Shamanic Journeys.

DELTA – 1.5-4 or less cycles per second – deep sleep

A simple meditation exercise is included for you to experiment with. Active meditation is a valuable tool that has been shown to reduce stress, and in so doing improves quality of life. There are many forms of meditation. This particular meditative technique is patterned on Transcendental Meditation without the personalized mantra. It is easy, effective, and with practice will benefit you on many levels.

NOTE: A person who is driving on a freeway, and discovers that they can't recall the last five miles, is often in a **theta** state – induced by the process of monotonous freeway driving. This can also occur in the shower or tub or even while shaving or brushing your hair. It is a state where tasks become so automatic that you can mentally disengage from them. The ideation that can take place during the **theta** state is often free flow and occurs without censorship or guilt. It is typically a very positive mental state.

Theta brain function state has been found to be active during Shamanic Journeys. Therefore breathing properly and meditation while not specifically "A Shamanic Way," they ARE critical tools for developing effective Shamanic work.

RECIPE 10:

For Living a Full & Blessed Life

Everyday:

1. *Do something for yourself.*
2. *Do something for another.*
3. *Do something mental.*
4. *Do something physical.*
5. *Do something you don't want to do.*
6. *Count your blessings.*

Breathing

Life is one long series of breaths. Without breath we die. Without breathing properly we may experience a variety of discomforts and perhaps even dis-ease. The stress and pollution of our environment has caused the development of improper breathing. The act of breathing for full benefit is dependent on a variety of circumstances beyond the purity of the air we breathe. Our posture, whether standing, sitting, or walking is a significant contributor to correct breathing, as is our stress level.

Yoga breathing exercises not only restore a person's vital life force but reduce stress. By concentrating on your breath you put yourself into a meditative state and subsequently the chemicals that define your stress level will go down, your brain waves will change, and you will restore your vital life force.

Most people breathe from the top of their lungs at the collar bone level unless they pay attention and shift their breathing consciously to deeper in their lungs. It is the most energy wasting effort for the least benefit return.

Breathing is divided into **high**; the collar bone type, **mid**; breathing from the diaphragm pushing the ribs upward, and **low**; or abdominal breathing, and is a very beneficial type of breathing. Yogi Complete Breathing incorporates the qualities of all three types of breathing. This type of breathing gives maximum benefit to the entire respiratory system with minimum of effort.

You will find several examples of breathing exercises following this explanation. The Complete Breathing Technique, Rhythmic Breathing, and the Cleansing Breath all provide you with the basics for breathing in a beneficial manner. Yoga breathing is very effective in activating the energetic body and healing in addition to raising your inner Spirit. The last example is a breathing/meditation combination exercise that incorporates and activates the Lightbody that we have within us.

Journal Page

RECIPES FOR BREATHING

- **Complete Breathing**
- **Circular Breathing**
- **Rhythmic Breathing**
- **Cleansing Breath**

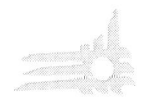

Breathe

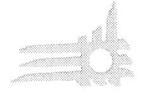

RECIPE 11:

COMPLETE BREATHING TECHNIQUE

INHALE

1. Fill the lower part of the lungs from the diaphragm, thus pushing forward the front walls of the abdomen.
2. Fill the mid part of the lungs, pushing out the lower ribs, breast-bone, and chest.
3. Fill the higher portion of the lungs, lifting the upper chest including the upper ribs and collarbone.
4. This last part will also cause the abdomen to slightly draw in.

EXHALE

5. Exhale slowly slightly drawing in your abdomen and slightly lifting it, exhale fully and slowly.
6. When the lungs are completely emptied start your inhale again.

NOTE: The COMPLETE BREATHING TECHNIQUE holds true for all breathing whether as an exercise as described or just as you go about your day. With practice that type of COMPLETE BREATHING will become normal for you without effort, as it was when you were a baby. Repeat the Complete Breathing exercise as often as you desire. You will find with practice that this becomes very easy.

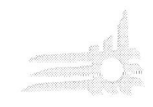

RECIPE 12:

CIRCULAR BREATHING TECHNIQUE

(See the central figures in the Illustration for counterclockwise sequence: top left, down, up right, return to starting position.) (You can do a search for Circular Breathing on the internet.)

The process as outlined below is a continuous inhalation and exhalation or circular breathing without pause until energy shift takes place or you are just "done". Utilize the Complete Breathing Technique described in Recipe 16.

INHALE

1. Sit or stand in an erect position, feet together.
2. Extend your arms straight out from your body.
3. Bring hands together and interlock your fingers.
4. Bend your arms and place your interlocked hands under your chin.
5. Rest your chin on your interlocked hands and
6. Inhale steadily and slowly through your nose, dropping your head and gently pushing your chin against your interlocked hands. As you are inhaling slowly lift your elbows outward towards your ears bringing them to right angles to your shoulder level.

NOTE: At the peak of your inhale your elbows will be at right angles to your shoulders or higher (closer to your ears).

EXHALE

7. Exhale slowly blowing air out of your mouth. While exhaling gently push your head back with your interlocked hands allowing your elbows to come together, (they will be at right angles to your body) your head will be tipped back (you will be looking at the ceiling). As you do this gently bend backwards as far as you can easily go.

8. At the peak of your bending backwards allow your elbows to slowly drop to your chest, maintaining your interlocked hands against your chin and at the peak of your exhale you will be returned to your starting INHALE position.

9. Repeat the full process rhythmically and smoothly until you feel a shift in your energy or you are done.

Journal Page

Journal Page

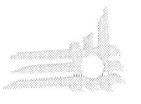

RECIPE 13:

RHYTHMIC BREATHING TECHNIQUE

(See the outside figures in the Illustration for counterclockwise sequence: top left, down, up right, return to starting position.) (You can do a search for Rhythmic Breathing on the internet.)

Rhythmic Breathing enhances the ability for healing and magnetic attraction, or the Law of Attraction. It is important that the time it takes for the inhalation is the same for exhalation.

1. Sit or stand in an erect position with hands loosely in your lap or at your sides and your feet comfortably together. Do not cross your legs if you are sitting.
2. Inhale steadily through your nose using the Complete Breathing Technique described in Recipe 16 raising arms up over your head.
3. Pause and hold your inhalation for a few seconds, six or eight seconds, whatever is comfortable.
4. Exhale slowly through your mouth, slightly drawing in your abdomen and slightly lifting it, exhale fully and slowly lowering your arms this may take a count of six, eight, or ten seconds until the lungs are completely empty.
5. Pause for a few seconds, six or eight seconds, whatever is comfortable.
6. At the end of your pause start your inhale again.

Repeat this Rhythmic Breathing exercise several times in each session. You will notice your capacity to increase the duration of your inhalation and exhalation will eventually be fifteen seconds. Keep your time for retention between breaths at half the time of the inhalation and exhalation. You will feel your body's vibration at a higher rate then when you started.

NOTE: You will feel yourself develop a graceful rhythm of raising and lowering your arms coordinated with your breath. Performing this breathing exercise you may notice your posture improve, your abdomen will tighten, and your energy will increase dramatically.

At the end of your Rhythmic Breathing session use a Cleansing Breath to refresh you. Speakers and singers may find this Cleansing Breath beneficial after their vocal/respiratory exertion.

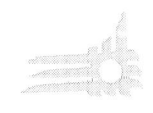

RECIPE 14:

CLEANSING BREATH TECHNIQUE

1. Inhale a Complete Breath as described in Complete Breathing Technique.
2. Retain the air a few seconds.
3. Pucker your lips, as if to whistle, do not swell out your cheeks.
4. Exhale a small amount of air with vigor.
5. Pause.
6. Exhale a small amount of air with vigor.
7. Pause.
8. Repeat sequence until your lungs are completely exhaled.
9. Repeat sequence as many times as you feel is necessary.

Journal Page

MEDITATION

Meditation

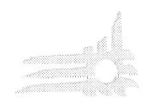

Simple Meditation

Try to do this before you eat something. Your meditation will be deeper if your body is not busy digesting a meal. We recommend meditating twice a day; when you first wake up, to start the day, and in the late afternoon. If you meditate too late in the day you will find you have too much energy to fall asleep at your regular time as meditating is a powerful energizer.

If you chose to live your life in A Shamanic Way you may want to do some type of inner work each day. If so, you may want to vary your routine of Journey Work with Meditation. Both techniques are valuable because their use will strengthen your abilities as a Shamanic practitioner.

Use your meditative state to reduce stress, to connect to your inner voice for answers, or to extend your energy to the world.

RECIPE 15:

SIMPLE MEDITATION

NOTE: Make sure the telephone will not ring, and that children or animals will not interrupt you. Typically meditation guidance tells us to meditate for 20 minutes two times a day to trigger a change in your mind, body, energy, and spirit connection. We say to you, this is a personal choice. Meditate as long and as frequently as is comfortable.

1. Find a comfortable place to sit.

NOTE: Leaning back against something is OK. You can put your feet up on a stool or another chair if you want. The important thing is to be comfortable. If you are not comfortable your thoughts will be consumed by your "uncomfortableness".

Keeping your feet or legs crossed will retain your energy for yourself, if you separate your feet your energy will go out to the community and the world.

2. Keep your back straight and your head free, in other words do not lie down or rest your head on the back of a chair or against a wall.
3. Take three slow deep breaths from you abdomen and allow your eyes to close.

NOTE: As your eyes close notice that your breathing will become more rhythmic and deeper.

4. On each exhale say or think the word "OM" holding it until your exhale is done.

A Shamanic Way

NOTE: This is a Sacred vibration that resonates in a positive way throughout the body.

When you say or think the word "OM" feel the vibration come from your abdomen up your spine and through the centerline of your neck, your head, and out the crown chakra, the top of your head. Make the "OM" sound a very round sound.

This activates the pineal gland, which is in the center of your head roughly located in the middle of the brain. This is the "door" for accessing Spirit.

With each exhale think or say the "OM", feeling the vibration move up your spine and out the top of your head, and feel yourself sink a little deeper like drifting down as on a bubble.

The sound/vibration of "OM" is a vehicle for deepening your meditative state and switching your brain waves to alpha waves.

You will notice your mind drifting to other things: What to have for dinner? Did I pay that bill? etc. There is no way to make your mind a blank. It is an "impossible task". Go ahead and think your thought through or until you are bored with thinking about it. If you have an itch scratch it, if you need to shift your position do so. Then gently and easily let yourself drift back to your breathing and the sound and the feel of the vibration of "OM" on each exhale.

5. You will become restless, go ahead and persevere for another few minutes.

NOTE: There will be a point where you feel like you are so deep you feel disconnected from your arms and legs. This does not mean they are numb, just that you are in a very deep meditative state. That point only lasts for a few minutes or even seconds. YOU ARE IN MEDITATION. Hold that state for as long as you can.

6. When you feel you are done, take a shallow breath and gently become aware of your surroundings.

7. Take another shallow breath and notice the sounds surrounding you.

8. Take another shallow breath and notice the position of your body.

9. Take another shallow breath gently move your fingers, toes, neck, back, etc.

10. Take another shallow breath and gently open your eyes. Look at your surroundings and note that your consciousness has returned to present awareness.

NOTE: If you choose you may want to journal at this time. Capturing the insights and information gained in a meditative state is often difficult after a period of time has elapsed between meditations and ***Remember***ing. It can be like a dream.

Journal Page

Journal Page

RECIPE 16:

> ### 'THE UNIFIED CHAKRA'
> ### Light Body Meditation

The Unified Chakra is the basic technique of Angelic Outreach. It supports your change at every level. The Unified Chakra creates a bubble of Light that allows you to handle vaster and vaster frequencies, and acts like a force field. It helps screen out other people's pictures of reality. Most of us walk around in other peoples' energies because our mental, emotional, energetic, spiritual and physical bodies are separated. The primary concern for Lightworkers is to unite our bodies and figure out just what is our energy.

The Unified Chakra is the best way we know of to assist you to follow your Spirit with every breath and every step. We suggest that you do the Unified chakra every single time that you notice that you are in the past or the future. At first that will seem like an incredible task, but if you will do it with discipline, you will find that within two weeks you will unify instantly. By the end of four to five weeks, you won't step out of the merged Unified state. Unlike a lot of meditations, you do not leave your body; you stay conscious. It is an altered state, but it is one that you can live in daily.

Before each stanza of "I breathe in light" fill your lungs and heart with life giving breath from your abdomen. Exhale as you invoke the words of each stanza. Feel the expansion of light around you with the progression of each stanza.

The "Unified Chakra Meditation" from What Is Lightbody? by Aliya Ziondra – Tashira Tachi-ren

I breathe in Light
Through the center of my heart
Opening my heart
Into a beautiful ball of Light
Allowing myself to expand

I breathe in Light
Through the center of my heart
Allowing the Light to expand
Encompassing my throat chakra
And my Solar plexus chakra
In one unified field of Light
Within, through, and around my body

I breathe in Light
Through the center of my heart
Allowing the Light to expand
Encompassing my brow chakra
And my navel chakra
In one unified field of Light
Within, through, and around my body

I breathe in Light
Through the center of my heart
Allowing the Light to expand
Encompassing my crown chakra
And my base chakra
In one unified field of Light
Within, through, and around my body

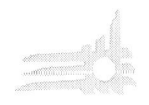

I breathe in Light
Through the center of my heart
Allowing the Light to expand
Encompassing my Alpha chakra (eight inches above my head)
And my Omega chakra (eight inches below my spine)
In one unified field of Light
Within, through, and around my body
I allow the Waves of Metatron
To move between these two points. **I AM** a unity of Light

I breathe in Light
Through the center of my heart
Allowing the Light to expand
Encompassing my eighth chakra (above my head)
And my upper thighs
In one unified field of Light
Within, through, and around my body
I allow my emotional body to merge
With my physical body. **I AM** a unity of Light

I breathe in Light
Through the center of my heart
Allowing the Light to expand
Encompassing my ninth chakra (Above my head)
And my lower thighs
In one unified field of Light
Within, through, and around my body
I allow my mental body to merge
With my physical body. **I AM** a unity of Light

I breathe in Light
Through the center of my heart
Allowing the Light to expand
Encompassing my tenth chakra
(Above my head)
And to my Knees
In one unified field of Light
Within, through and around my body
I allow my Spiritual body to merge
With my physical body
Creating the unified field. **I AM** a unity of Light

I breathe in Light
Through the center of my heart
Allowing the Light to expand
Encompassing my eleventh chakra
(Above my head)
And my upper calves
In one unified field of Light
Within, through and around my body
I allow the Oversoul to merge
With the unified field. **I AM** a unity of Light

I breathe in Light
Through the center of my heart
Allowing the Light to expand
Encompassing my twelfth chakra
(Above my head)
And my lower calves
In one unified field of Light
Within, through and around my body
I allow the Christ Oversoul to merge
With the unified field. **I AM** a unity of Light

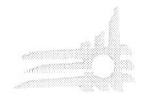

I breathe in Light
Through the center of my heart
Allowing the Light to expand
Encompassing my thirteenth chakra
(Above my head)
And my feet
In one unified field of Light
Within, through and around my body
I allow the I AM Oversoul to merge
With the unified field. **I AM** a unity of Light

I breathe in Light
Through the center of my heart
Allowing the Light to expand
Encompassing my fourteenth chakra
(Above my head)
And to below my feet
In one unified field of Light
Within, through and around my body
I allow the Source's Presence to move
Throughout the unified field. **I AM** a unity of Light

I breathe in Light
Through the center of my heart
I ask that the highest level of my spirit
Radiate forth from the center of my heart
Filling the unified field completely
I radiate forth throughout this day. **I AM** a unity of Spirit

Now ground yourself multi-dimensionally.

- Imagine a thick line of Light, beginning at the Omega chakra (eight inches below your spine), extending upwards through your spine and on upwards into the upper part of the unified field.

- Ground into the vastness of your own Spirit. Allow your Spirit to stabilize you. Now run twelve lines of light downward from the point of the Omega chakra, (eight inches below your spine) opening around your feet like a cone.

- You are not grounding into the earth. You are stabilizing yourself across the parallel realities of the planetary hologram.

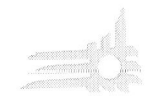

Journal Page

Journal Page

Chapter 9
THE BEGINNING

- **When to Start**
- **How to Start**
- **Where to Start**

You have all the pieces
You have the rhythm of the ritual
You have the gift
Now you have "YOU"

THE BEGINNING
Quick Guide

This is the place where everything in the book comes together. You will find that although what you have read so far may seem a bit overwhelming, we are here to tell you that living your life in A Shamanic Way can be as simple as paying attention and honoring the world around you or as elegant as formal ritual and ceremony. It is up to you. Everything in between those two extremes goes. Your imagination and dedication to your personal awakening of your inner Spirit is the only limitation.

We want to provide you with a quick guide of what is contained in this book for your convenience. This will allow you to quickly develop your own personal style without confusion or a lot of effort.

1. Sacred Smoke – Smudging (Tools, Space, People) – Cleanses and releases negative energy and thoughts. It prepares the space, Sacred tools, and people for the work.

2. Create Sacred Circle / Space – Defines a space of purity that will become a vortex of energy and blessings from above for spiritual work.

3. Invocation of the Directions – Invitation for help and support to the elements and powers inherent in the directions.

4. Journey Work – The work itself of gaining guidance and blessings from Spirit.

5. Chakra Balancing, Opening, and Aligning – Brings the energetic body into balance to create an optimum environment in the body to heal, perform healing, or gain

wisdom. With balanced chakras the process of journey work is much faster.

6. Ritual / Ceremony – To accomplish a spiritual goal.
7. Breathing / Meditation – Empowers your practice.

As you can see there is not that much to **_Remember_** now that you have been made aware of the process.

This book has a lot of information, but if after reading this book you only get the following you have accomplished a huge, huge step towards Awakening Your Inner Spirit.

1. The importance of **INTENTION**.
2. The importance of being in the **NOW.**
3. There is no **RIGHT** or **WRONG** way to perform any of the recipes and rituals in this book. This book is simply a guide to your personal awakening.

Final Words:
THE BEGINNING

- When to Start – anytime (as soon as you want – you don't need to be READY)
- How to Start – with honor and respect (having all the tools is not necessary)
- Where to Start – wherever you are comfortable (a place you will not be interrupted)

We are so excited that you are on this path now. We welcome you to *A Shamanic Way* of Awakening Your Inner Spirit.

Welcome Home!

Penny

P.S. If you have any questions journey on your question Spirit will provide you the answers and give you guidance.

For consultations contact Penny via her website, www.circleoneshamanichealing.com.

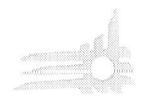

MEET THE AUTHOR
Penny

Penny Randall:

Becoming a Shamanic Healer and practitioner was never on my 'to do' list. It evolved over time and pressure from the Spirit and the Universe. My journey into Shamanic practice mirrors others who come into such an esoteric calling in the Western world. I was not born into it, nor was I a victim of a near death experience on the physical level. This is not to say that my experiences were always easy or even welcomed. Some were absolutely what one would call near-death experiences on an emotional and spiritual level. People, situations, and opportunities presented to me again and again over the years leading me into my current path.

As I worked with people on a Soul and Spiritual level I knew that without changing thought patterns and habits there was always a risk for them to fall back into situations that caused the need for Soul and Spirit work in the first place. As a certified hypnotherapist, a Reiki practitioner, ordained minister, author, and artist I combine these modalities with my Shamanic work; being guided by Spirit for the benefit of my clients. As I grow in my knowledge I apply that knowledge in my practice.

This book is a result of that experience of giving in to Spirit's guidance.

Welcome to *A Shamanic Way – Rituals, Rattles, and Recipes for Awakening Your Inner Spirit.*

Glossary

Altar – is the place the Shaman holds sacred tools and the place that connects with the spiritual world. When an altar is working correctly creates a tunnel of energy, light, linking the physical world with the spiritual world.

Bear Dance Ceremony – Healing ceremony practiced by the Native Americans celebrating the Spirit of the Bear. The dancers are Shamans that have the blessing of carrying the Bear medicine, which is believed to be a powerful healing medicine for the people. Many people attend for personal healing.

Calling In – Invitation or Invocation.

Ceremony/Ritual – Ceremonies & rituals are a means of celebration to welcome Spirit or God into your life or to mark a special occasion.

Chakras – Portals for the energy of the Universe to enter our body, activating it, healing it, energizing it. Different traditions say that we have different numbers of chakras, for purposes of our book we have chosen the system of seven most commonly known chakras.

Cord Cutting – A process done through a Shamanic journey. Cutting and clearing away the cords (connections) that connect us to people, places, and things that are unhelpful and binding in detrimental ways.

Core Shamanism – The process of "journey" that is practiced globally without any ritual or ceremony of cultural influence.

Creator or God – Every person calls differently to the Creativity of the Universe or God. Different spiritual traditions give different names: Jesus, Allah, Jehovah, Buddha, Wankam-Thankan, Ometeo, Baba, and so on. Our book <u>A Shamanic Way</u> simply used the words Creator and God to refer to this Magnificent Being inside and outside of us. Feel free to change the word Creator or God to your word for that Divine Being with whom you have your own spiritual relationship and with whom you feel good.

Curandero/Curandera or Gente de Conocimiento – A Mexican Shaman; see Shaman.

Directions – For purposes of our book we have chosen the system of eight directions. The four cardinal directions: North, East, South, West and four spirit based directions: Above, Below, Within, and Around – First and Always. These have powerful energy and are invited to help create Sacred Space. Other traditions and cultures have more or less than these eight.

Drum and Drumming – The round shape of the drum symbolizes the roundness of earth. The drum beat is the heart beat of the Universe.

EGO – Our personality and connection with our physical body. It generates the mental chatter we all live with day in and day out and unfortunately that chatter tends to be negative. The Ego tries to keep us stuck in the past or worrying about the future.

Elements – Earth, water, fire and air. These have powerful energy and are invited to help create Sacred Space.

Energetic body/lightbody – The invisible electromagnetic field that animates the body.

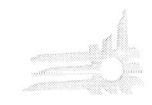

Extraction – A process done through a Shamanic journey to remove any unhelpful energy that enters the emptiness resulting from soul loss.

Gente de Conocimiento or Curandero/curandera – A Mexican Shaman; see Shaman.

Inner Spirit – That place inside of each of us that holds the answers to our questions, calms our emotions and, body, and the place that connects us to everything and everyone else in the Universe.

Intention – Your objective for your Journey, ceremony, or other work sent out to the Universe, Creator, or whatever you chose to call that higher good.

Invocation – Invitation.

Journey or Journey Work – The act of entering a trance state allowing access to the Spirit world; typically Theta brain wave activity takes place.

Kingdoms – Animal, mineral, plant, and human. These are honored and respected during any Shamanic ritual. And of course in living life in A Shamanic Way.

Lightworkers – Those actively connecting with their energetic and spiritual bodies and the connections to all things, visible and invisible, recognizing that all things are an energetic vibration.

Medicine bag/Sacred tool kit – Holds items that are close to your heart and items that pertain to a specific Shamanic task, whatever that may be for you.

Meditation – The act of calming the mind and moving the brain waves out of the Beta wave of waking state into the Alpha wave.

Power Animals – Similar to Spirit Guides but in the form of an animal, sometimes a fantasy type animal. Shamanic journey work allows conscious access to be established.

Prayer Stick – A decorated and blessed stick dedicated to holding your prayers or "holding space" for you.

Prayer Ties – A sequence of tied bundles of tobacco, typically twenty-two, forty-four, or sixty-six prayer ties which will anchor and hold your prayers beyond the time of your actual ritual.

Sacred Circle – Sacred Space is often delineated as a circle.

Sacred Smoke – Fragrant herbs, resins, and plants; when burned are allowed to smoke and change the energetic field of one being smudged, whether a person, a place, a business, a car, or just about anything.

Sacred Space – A dedicated space in which to do Sacred work be it a Shamanic journey, meditation, ritual or ceremony, or anything that is considered very special requiring dedicated respected space.

Sacred Tools – Items that are close to your heart, and items that pertain to a specific Shamanic task, whatever that may be for you.

Self-igniting Charcoal – Tablets of charcoal that will continue to burn after lighting just a small part such as the edge of the tablet.

Shaman / Shamanic Practitioner – A person who has the ability to travel to the Spiritual World at will becoming a bridge or a messenger between the physical world and the Spiritual World.

Smudging – Wafting Sacred Smoke over a person, place, or thing cleansing the energetic body of any negative energy that may have been picked up.

Soul Retrieval – An elaborate ritual to invite back soul pieces that have left due to trauma, illness, or other upsetting events. The Shamanic healer "journeys" and lost soul pieces that want to come back and be helpful are invited to "return home" to the person being healed.

Spirit Guides – Entities that accompany us on our journey of life. Shamanic journey work allows conscious access to be established.

Sun Dance – Healing ceremony practiced by the Native Americans. The difference between the Bear Dance and the Sun Dance is significant. Although both are for healing; the Bear Dance is for healing of the people; the Sun Dance is for healing of the earth and all the kingdoms; animal, plant, mineral, and human.

Totem – Typically a Power Animal in the form of an animal, but can be anything physical or non-physical. Shamanic journey work allows conscious access to be established.

Unified Chakra – A meditation specific to creating a. bubble of Light within, through, and around your body, facilitating higher vibrational frequencies. Acts like a force field against absorption of other energies. A practice for staying in the present.

Wingmen – Guardians of the ceremonies in Native American traditions. Protects the people and the sacred space.

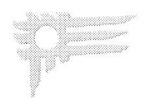

Index

A

Adrenals 111, 126
Akashic Records 96
Albahaca (basil) 45
Altar 33, 51, 138, 141, 196
Altar Space 138
Altered state 11, 83, 133, 182
Ancestors 68, 72
Angels 11, 84, 96
Animal kingdom 4
Ascended masters 84
Aura 141
Awareness xii, 90, 97, 114, 116, 119–120, 133, 157, 179

B

Bear 61, 67, 73, 76, 111, 119, 126, 196, 200
Bear Dance Ceremony 196
Being in the moment 140
Blessed life 159
Body 11, 13, 16, 21, 25, 32, 42, 52, 103–104, 110–111, 114, 116, 121, 141, 144, 156–157, 161, 166–167, 171, 176–179, 182–186, 191, 196–198, 200
Body, emotional 184
  Body, energetic 13, 21, 24, 111, 144, 156, 161, 191, 200
  Body, mental 184
  Body, physical 110, 114, 141, 184–185, 197
  Body, spiritual 185
Brain waves 156, 160, 178, 199

Breath 24, 86, 145, 156, 160, 164, 171–172, 179, 182
Breathing, circular 166
  Breathing, cleansing 166
  Breathing, Complete 160, 163, 165–166, 170, 172
  Breathing, Rhythmic 160, 163, 170–171
Bridge xi, 101, 112–113, 155, 199
Buffalo 60, 64, 72, 76, 109, 126

C

California Bay 26
Call back 89, 91, 95
Calling in the Directions 25, 32, 49, 51–52, 58–60, 64
Cardinal directions 25, 39, 44, 51, 56, 134, 197
Cedar 22, 26, 148
Ceremony xiii, 3–5, 27, 39, 43–44, 51, 56–59, 131, 133, 138, 140, 142, 191–192, 196, 198–200
Chakra balancing 13, 191
Chakras 101–104, 107–109, 111–114, 116–118, 121, 141, 144–145, 192, 196
Change patterns 16
Circular Breathing 166
Cleansing 21, 24, 26, 31, 155, 160, 163, 171–172, 200
Cleansing Breath 155, 160, 163, 171–172
Closing 57, 139, 150
Complete Breathing 155, 160, 163, 165–166, 170, 172

201

Connecting to energy 24
Conscious xii, 97, 182, 199–200
Conscious awareness xii
Copal 22, 27
Cord cutting 13, 15, 196
Cords and webs 16
Core shamanism 3–4, 11, 196
Cosmic connection 70, 74
Cosmic will 63, 74, 76, 101
Cougar 116, 120, 127
Creator 27, 62, 83, 196–198
Crown chakra 112, 117, 145, 178, 183
Curandero/Curandera 197–198
Cypress 26

D

Deep meditation 11
Deer 110, 118, 126
Directions 25, 32, 39, 43–44, 49–52, 55–60, 62, 64, 76, 89, 96–97, 103, 118, 134, 138–139, 191, 197
Disassociation 14
Divorce 16
Dolphin 115, 119, 126
Drum 19, 22, 31, 43, 58, 89, 95, 134, 144, 197
Drumming 11–12, 51, 58, 83, 89, 94, 134, 144–145, 148, 197

E

Eagle 60, 65, 72, 76, 117, 120, 127
Earthbound spirits 85
East 25, 39, 49, 51, 62, 65, 76–77, 111, 126, 134, 144, 197
Ego xii, 107–108, 136, 197
Electromagnetic 141, 156, 197
Elements 4, 27, 31, 191, 197
Emotional body 184
Endocrine gland 104, 126

Energetic body 11, 13, 21, 24, 111, 144, 156, 161, 191, 197, 200
Energetic body/lightbody 197
Energy xii, xiii, 3–5, 9, 11, 13, 15–16, 21, 24–26, 37, 39, 42–45, 51, 56–59, 62, 64–65, 68, 74, 76, 83, 85–87, 89, 94, 101, 103–104, 111–112, 114–116, 118, 131, 133, 136, 141–142, 144–145, 148–150, 156, 160, 166–167, 171, 176–177, 182, 191, 196–198, 200
Energy channels 13
Energy clearing 131, 133, 141, 144, 150
Energy Clearing for a Person 144
Energy grid realignment 13
Energy ties 13
Energy work xiii, 5
Ether 74, 119
Ethical integrity xiii
Exorcisms 97
Extraction 1, 13, 15–16, 198

F

Fanning 25
Father Sky 27, 62, 68, 74, 76
Fear 15, 66, 89, 108, 110, 115, 117, 126, 139
Feather 25, 144–145
Feel the energy 25, 42, 86
Feminine spirit 62, 69, 73
Fennel 26
Five bodies 104
Focus 37, 56–57, 65, 85, 111, 131, 141

G

Gente de Conocimiento 197–198
Great Mystery 63, 71, 74
Grid 13, 141

H

Healing xi–xiii, 1, 3, 11, 13–15, 26–27, 63, 66, 76, 85, 103, 111, 113, 118, 121, 134, 161, 170, 191, 196, 200
Healing work xii, 11, 85, 103, 111, 121
Heart anchor 74
Heart chakra 101, 104–105, 112–113, 115
Higher being 84
House Blessing 133, 150

I

Illness xi, 14, 200
Inner Self 84, 86, 108
Inner spirit xi, 3–5, 12, 103, 156, 161, 191–193, 195, 198
Inner voice 33, 63, 70, 127, 176
Intention xii, 3, 22, 24, 26, 31–32, 37, 43, 51–52, 56, 58–59, 62, 81, 85–86, 88–89, 91, 94–97, 133–134, 136, 138–140, 145, 148–149, 198
Intuition xiii, 114, 116, 120

J

Journaling xiv
Journey 11–15, 31, 33, 67, 81, 83–85, 88–89, 91–92, 94–97, 104, 120, 133, 139, 176, 191–193, 195–196, 198–200
Journey work 33, 85, 88–89, 139, 176, 191–192, 198–200
Juniper 26

K

Kingdoms 4, 198, 200
Kingdoms, Animal 4

L

Lessons xii, 66, 120
Light body 182
Limpias 97
Lost soul parts 16, 84
Lower world 81, 83–84, 88–91, 94, 96–97

M

Magic 12, 136
Medicine bag 33, 198
Medicine plants 26
Medicine plants for smudging 26
Meditation 11, 52, 116, 133, 155–158, 161, 175–179, 182–183, 192, 199–200
Mental body 184
Mental level xi
Messenger xi, 199
Methods for Cleansing Sacred Tools 31
Mexican Tradition 45
Middle world 81, 84–85, 97, 111
Mint 26
Mitakuye Oyasin 63, 69–70, 74, 76
Mother Earth 27, 42, 62, 69, 73, 76, 109, 118
Mugwort 26, 45
Mullein 27

N

Native American Traditions 5, 200
Nature 5, 12, 83
Negative energies 15, 97
Non-ordinary reality 3, 83, 88, 92, 97, 134
North 25, 49, 51, 59, 62, 64, 76–77, 109, 126, 134, 197

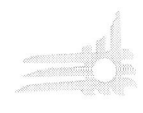

O

Om 177–178
Omega Chakra 184, 187
Ordinary reality 3, 16, 83, 88, 92, 95, 97, 134
Ovaries/Testes 109

P

Parallel reality 84
Personal awakening 191, 193
Personal Power 84, 111–112, 119, 121, 126
Physical body 110, 114, 141, 184–185, 197
Physical level 104, 121
Physical world xi, 60, 76, 113, 115, 196, 199
Pineal gland 178
Pirul (pepper tree) 45
Plant energy 26
Plant kingdom 24
Power animals 11, 83–84, 90–91, 94–95, 101, 103, 118–119, 121, 126, 199–200
Power direction 52
Power Song 4, 84
Prayer 19, 22, 27, 71, 76–77, 131, 133–134, 138–141, 150, 199
Prayer Ties 138, 140, 199
Prodigiosa (mugwort) 45
Prosperity 150
Protection 27, 37
Psychic ability xiii, 116
Psychotropic Drugs 12

R

Rattling 12, 58, 83, 89, 134, 145, 148
Recipe 24, 37, 42, 44, 49, 51, 57, 59–60, 64, 72, 76, 81, 86, 131, 136, 140, 155, 159, 165–166, 170, 172, 177, 182
Recipes xi, xii, 3–5, 12, 40, 44, 52, 103, 138, 192, 195
Rhythmic Breathing 160, 163, 170
Rituals xi, xii, 3–5, 11–15, 19, 21–22, 25–26, 39–40, 43–44, 49, 51–52, 56–59, 81, 83, 103, 131, 133–134, 136, 138–140, 142, 149–150, 156, 190–192, 195–196, 198–200
Role of the Shaman xi
Ruda (Rue) 45

S

Sacred circle 37–40, 42–45, 138–140, 144, 191, 199
Sacred cord 63, 70, 74, 76
Sacred intention 26
Sacred Medicine 31
Sacred Smoke 19–22, 24–25, 31, 33, 43, 51, 56, 89, 94, 138–142, 148–149, 191, 199–200
Sacred Space 19, 26, 30–33, 39, 43–45, 51–52, 58, 76, 139, 141, 144, 197, 199
Sacred Tools 3, 19, 30–32, 39, 44, 51, 56, 58, 156, 191, 196, 198–199
Sage 26, 148
Self-Igniting Charcoal 22, 24, 199
Shaman xi, xii, 2–5, 14, 196–199
Shamanic healer xiii, 11, 14, 195, 200
Shamanic healing 1, 11, 13–14
Shamanic journey 12, 14–15, 83, 156–158, 196, 198–200
Shamanic practice xi, xiv, 3–4, 51, 92, 103, 111, 121, 195
Shamanic state of consciousness 11–12, 16
Shamanic tool kit 33

Shamanic way xi–xiv, 1, 3–5, 9–10, 12, 39–40, 52, 59, 92, 103, 134, 141, 146, 156, 158, 176, 191, 193, 195, 197–198
Shamanic work 11, 21, 31, 33, 83, 97, 139, 158
Shamanism xiv, 3, 5, 9, 83, 134, 196
Shaman's world 2
Skills 3
Smudging 4, 19, 21, 24–26, 31, 43, 51, 56, 58, 191, 200
Solar plexus 104, 107, 111–112, 119, 126, 183
Song, Power 4, 84
Songs 3, 51, 58, 134
Song, Smudging 4
Soul xi, 1, 11, 13–16, 84, 97, 101, 111, 131, 195, 198, 200
Soul loss 14–16, 198
Soul Retrieval 1, 11, 13–16, 200
South 25, 49, 51, 61–62, 66, 73, 76–77, 110, 126, 134, 197
Spirit xi, 3–5, 9, 11–12, 14, 19, 22, 24, 26–27, 32–33, 39, 51–52, 56, 58, 61–70, 73, 76, 82–85, 88, 90–91, 94–96, 103, 112, 114, 117, 120–121, 127, 131, 133–134, 138, 140–142, 145, 155–156, 161, 177–178, 182, 186–187, 191–193, 195–200
Spirit garden 26
Spirit guides 11, 33, 39, 52, 84, 90–91, 94–96, 199–200
Spirit realm 85
Spirits 57, 59–63, 67, 84–85
Spiritual body 185
Spiritual directions 25
Spirit world 4, 11–12, 14, 88, 133–134, 198
Stones 32, 58

Stress release 177
Subconscious mind 11, 92, 97
Sun Dance 140, 200
Sweet grass 22, 26–27

T

Teachers 83, 96
The Beginning 63, 67, 76, 190–191, 193
Third Eye 104, 112, 114, 116, 127
Three Worlds 82–85
Thymus 105
Tobacco 22, 27, 138, 148, 199
Toning 145
Totems 76, 83
Transcendental Meditation 157

U

Unified Chakra 182, 200
Universal Mind 63
Upper World 81, 84, 96–97
Uva Ursi 27

V

Vital life force 14, 68, 76, 160

W

West 25, 49, 51, 61–62, 67, 73, 76–77, 113, 126, 134, 144, 197
Wolf 113, 119, 126

Y

Yerba Santa 27

Printed in Great Britain
by Amazon